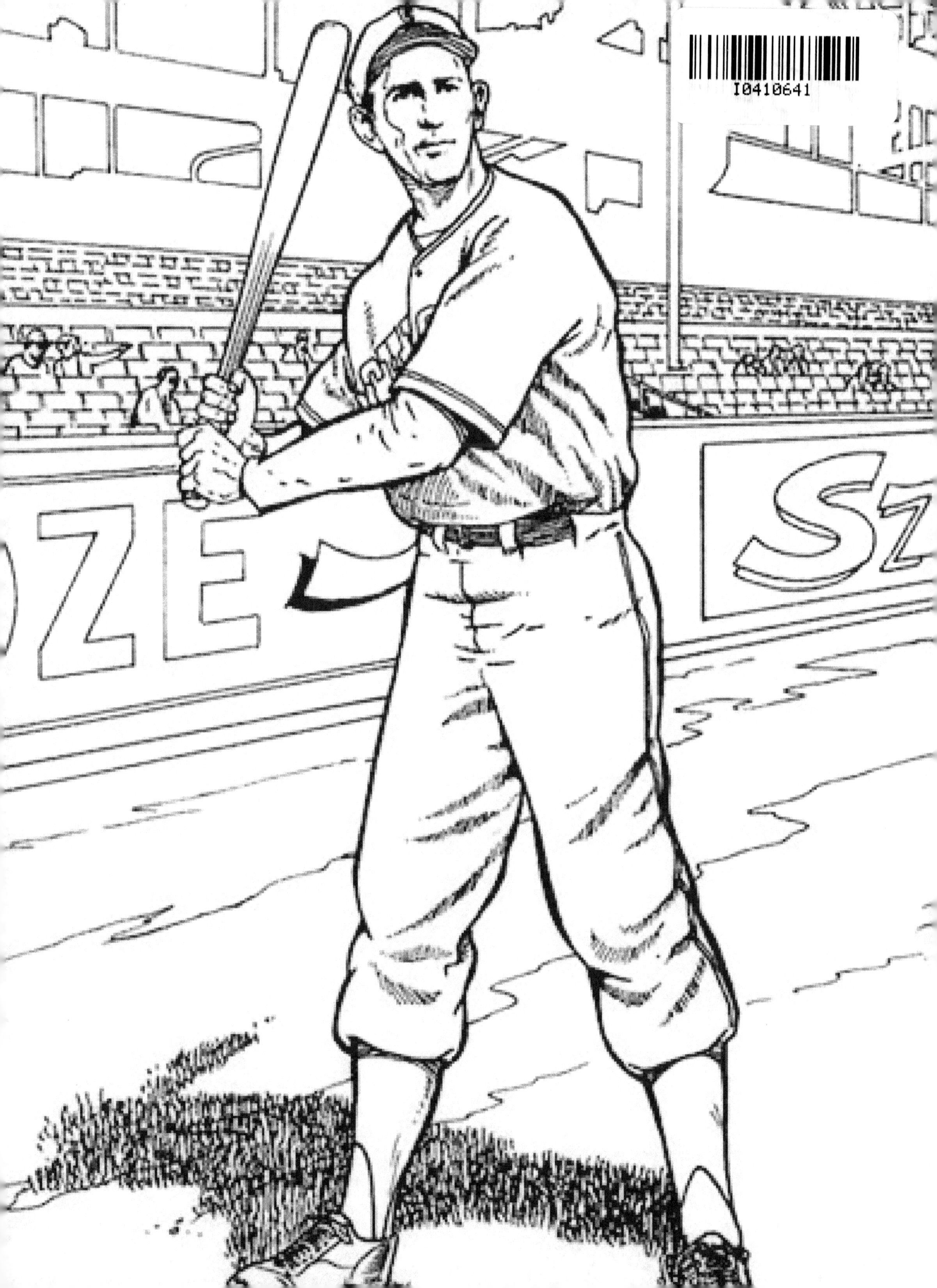
ZE
Sz

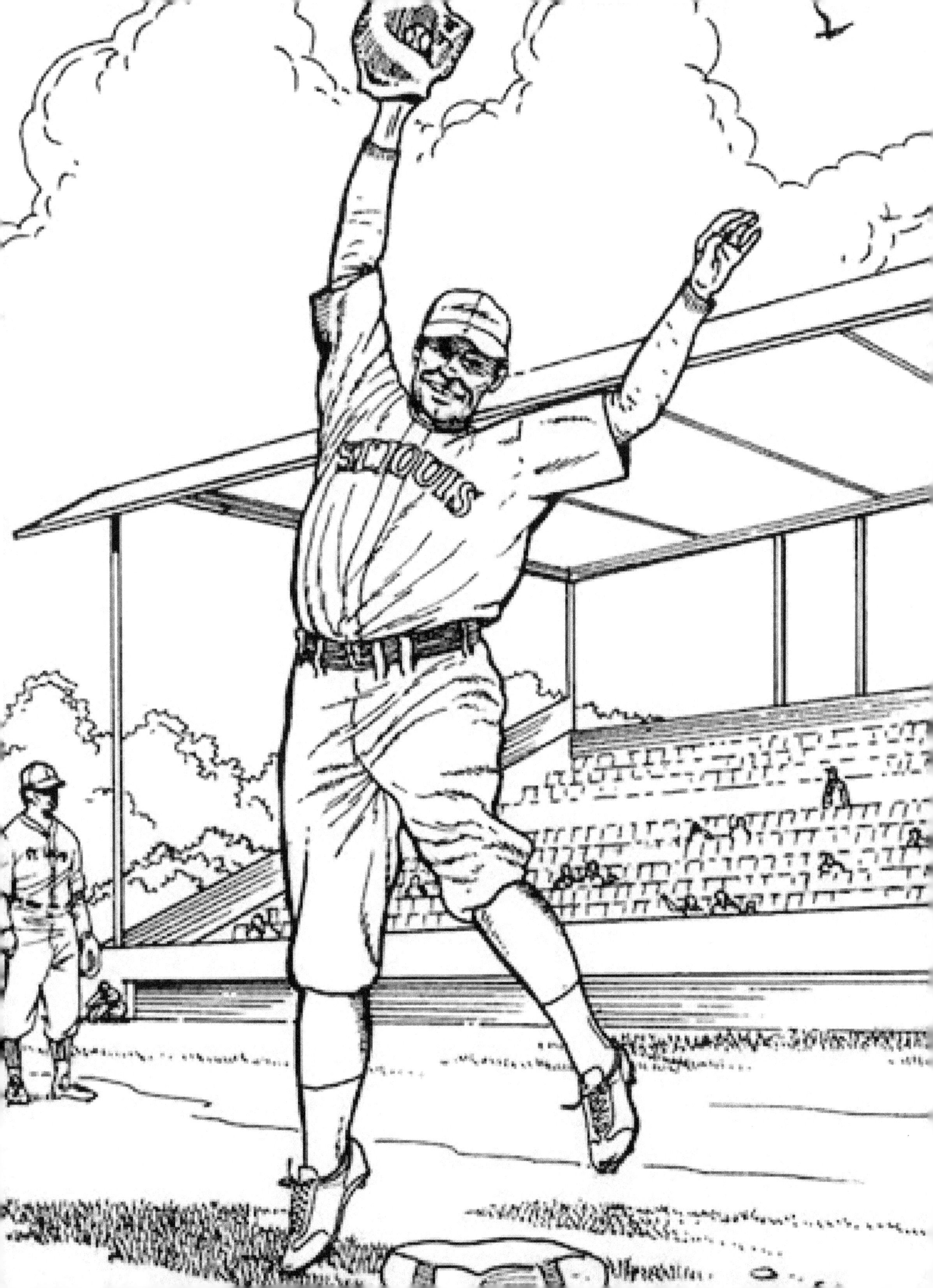
ST. LOUIS

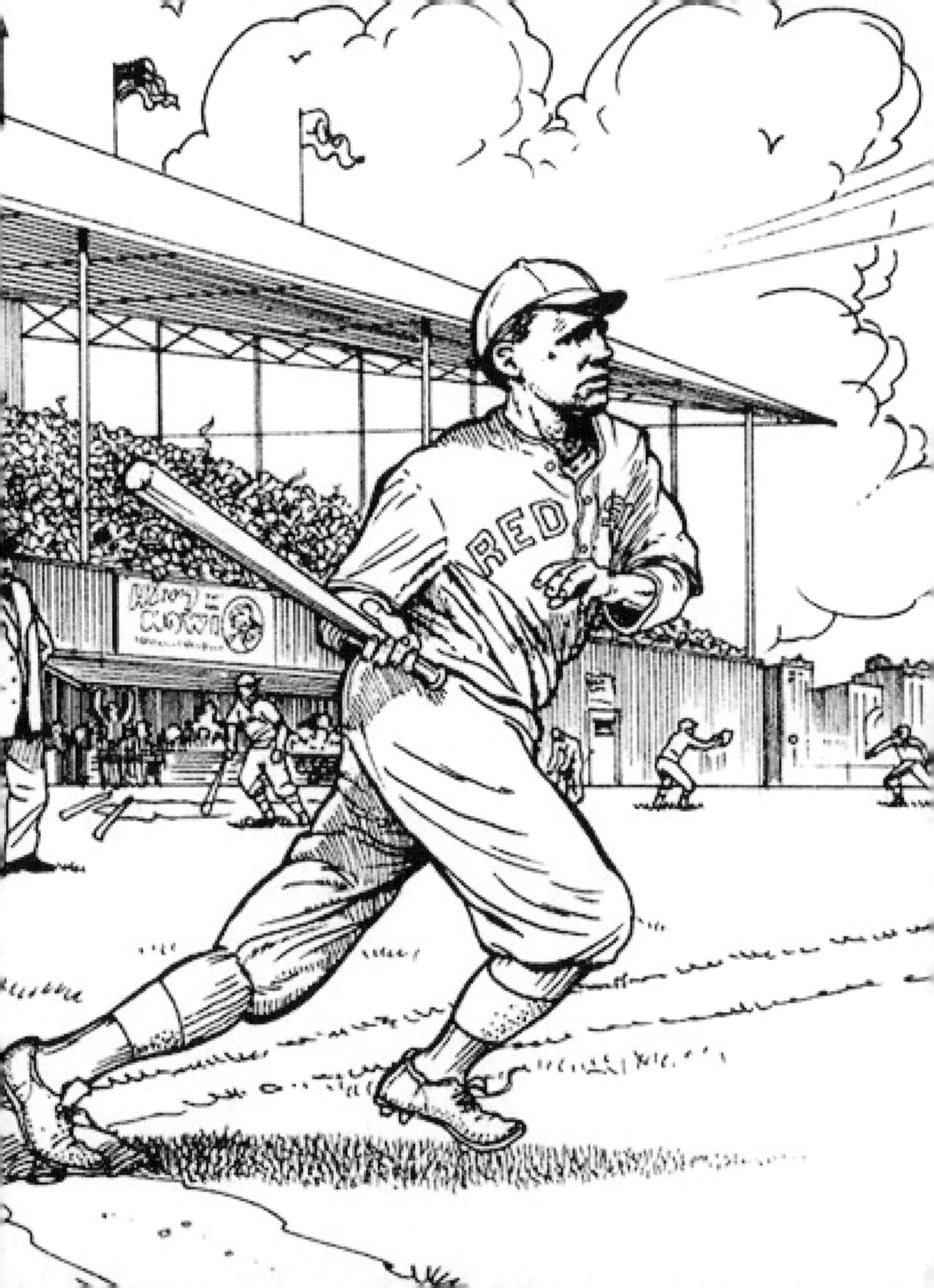
RED

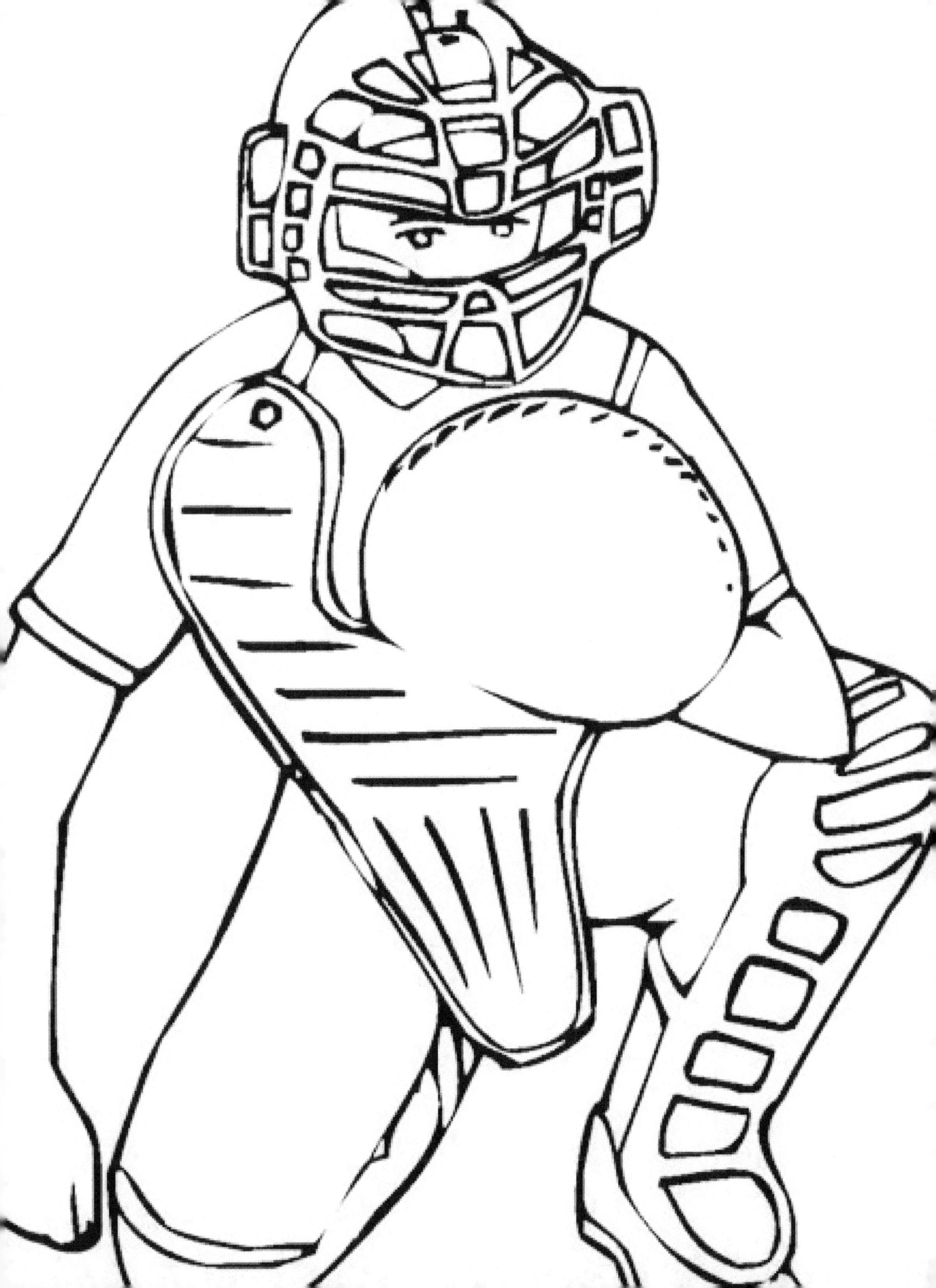

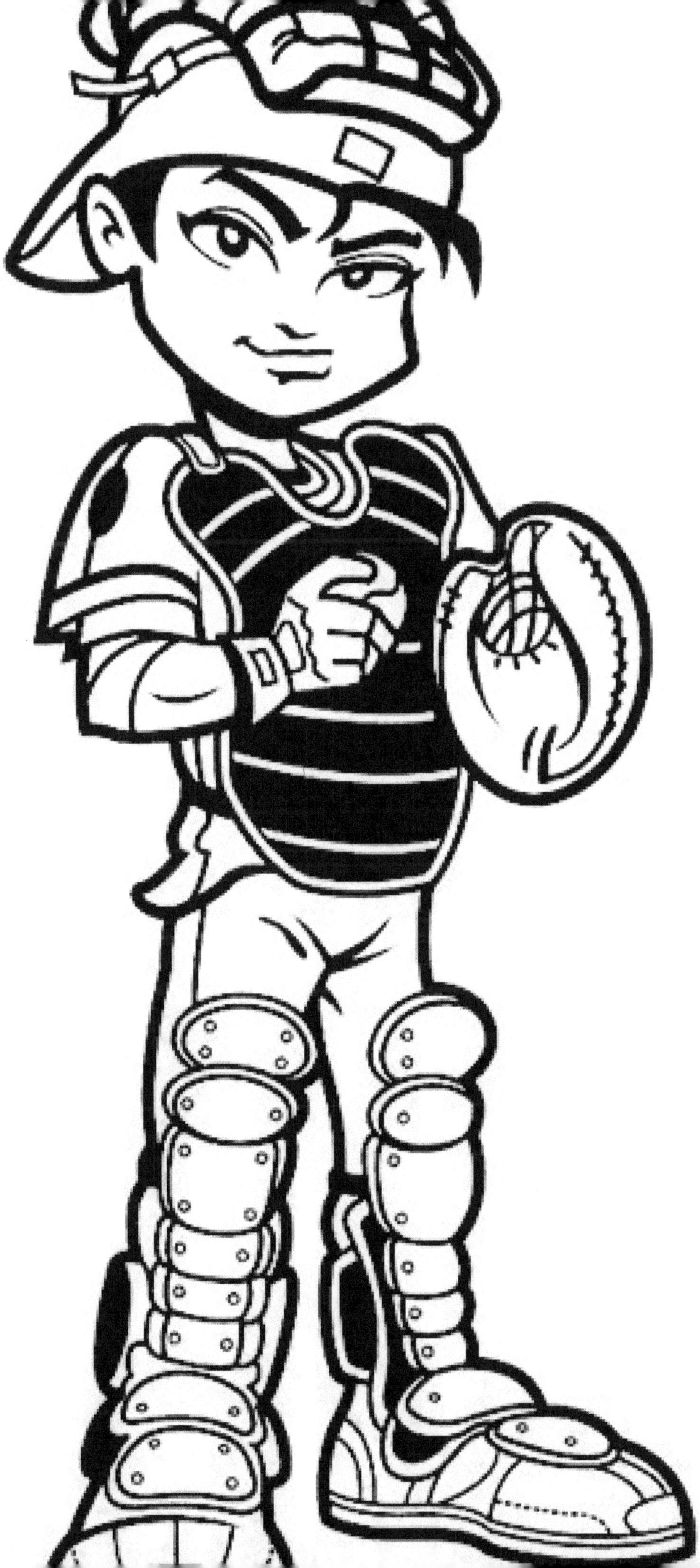

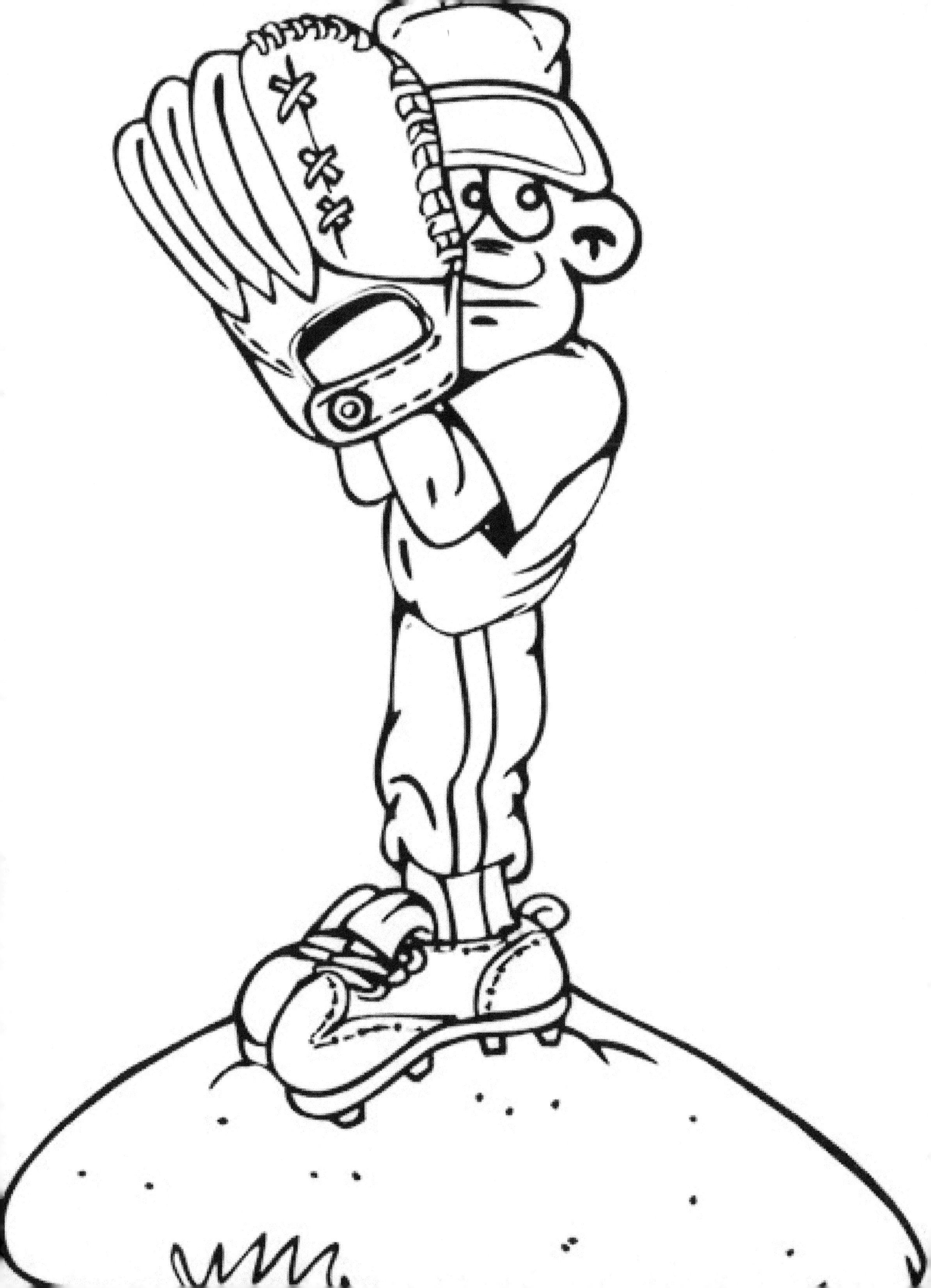

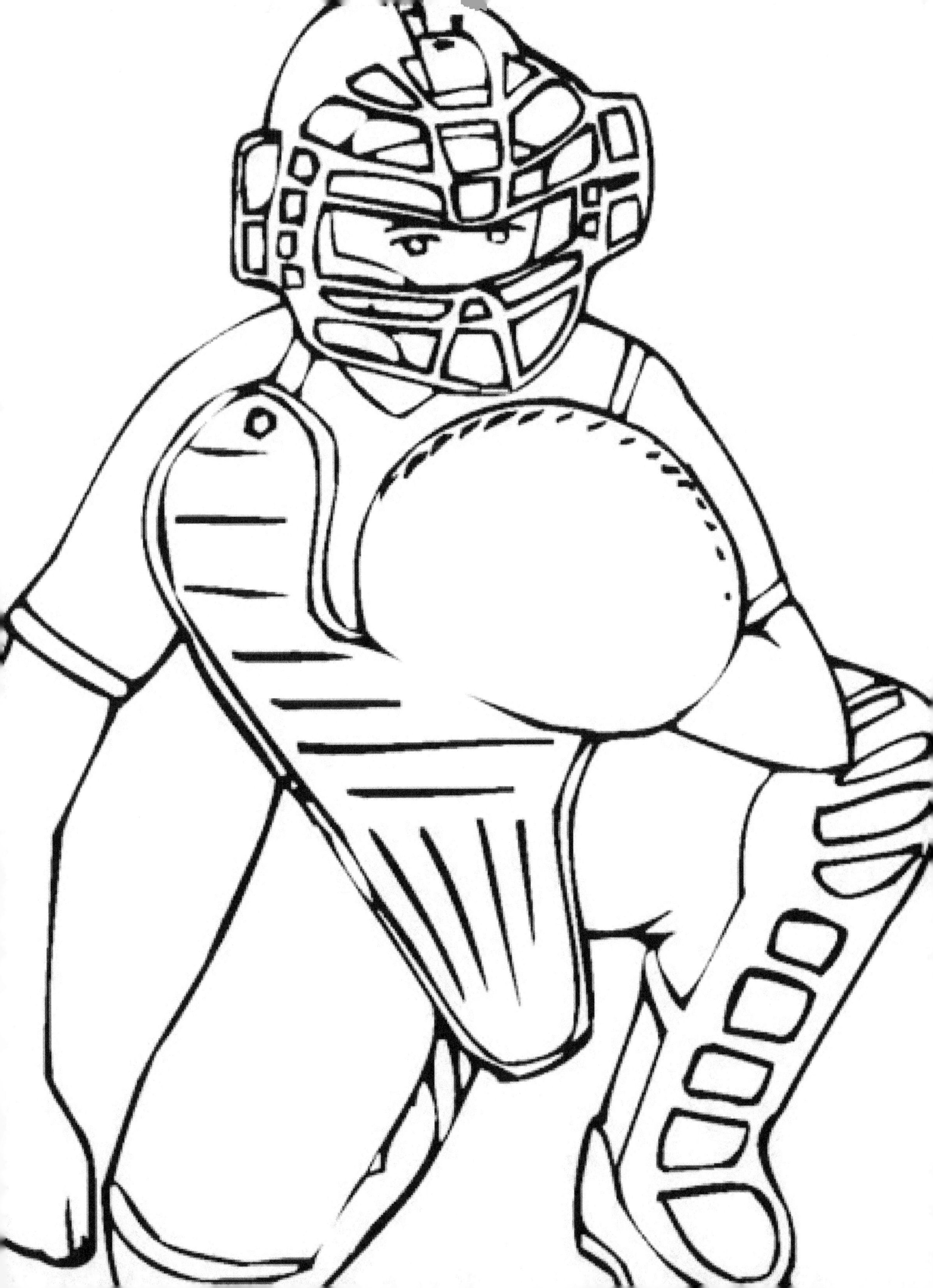

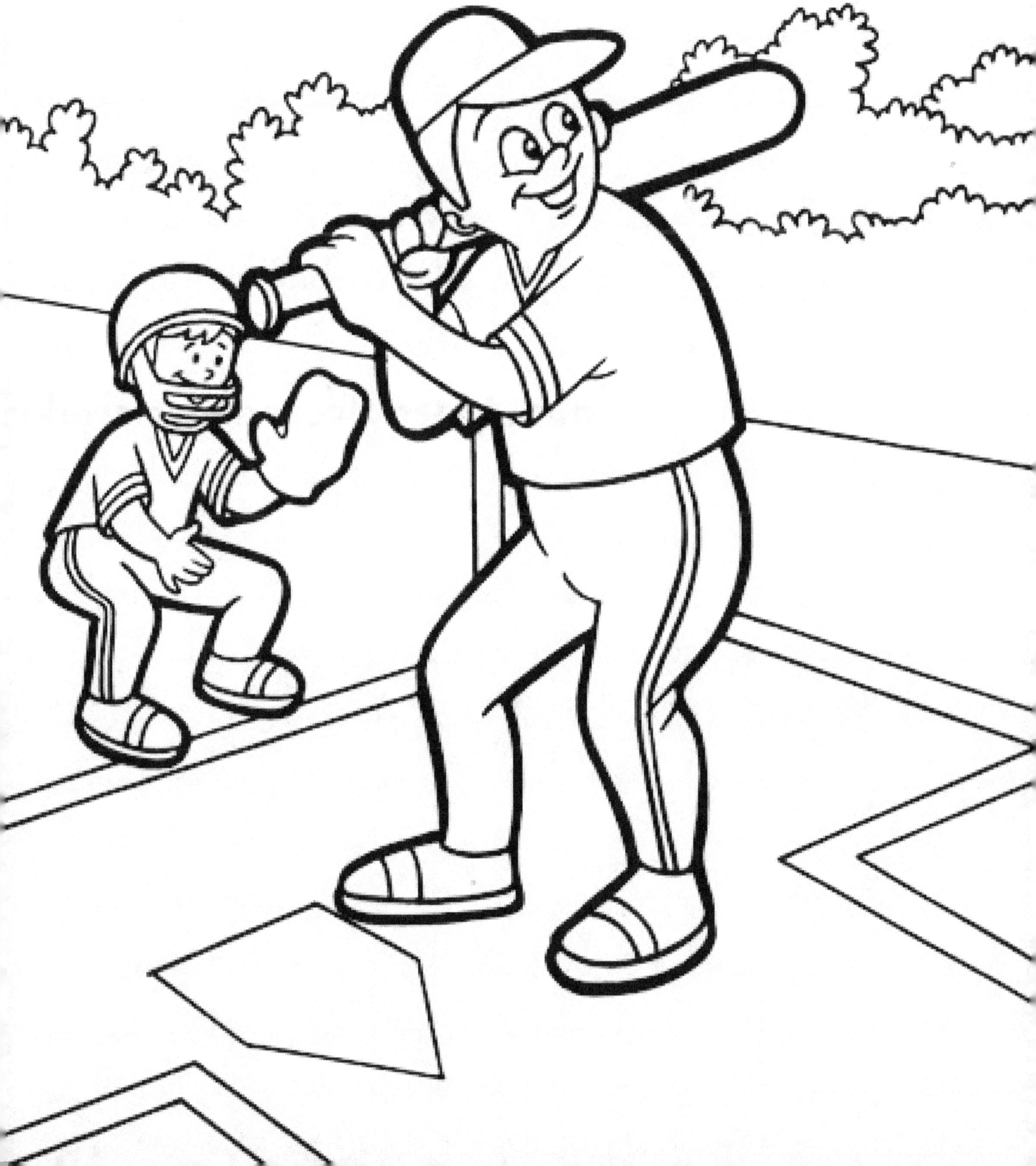

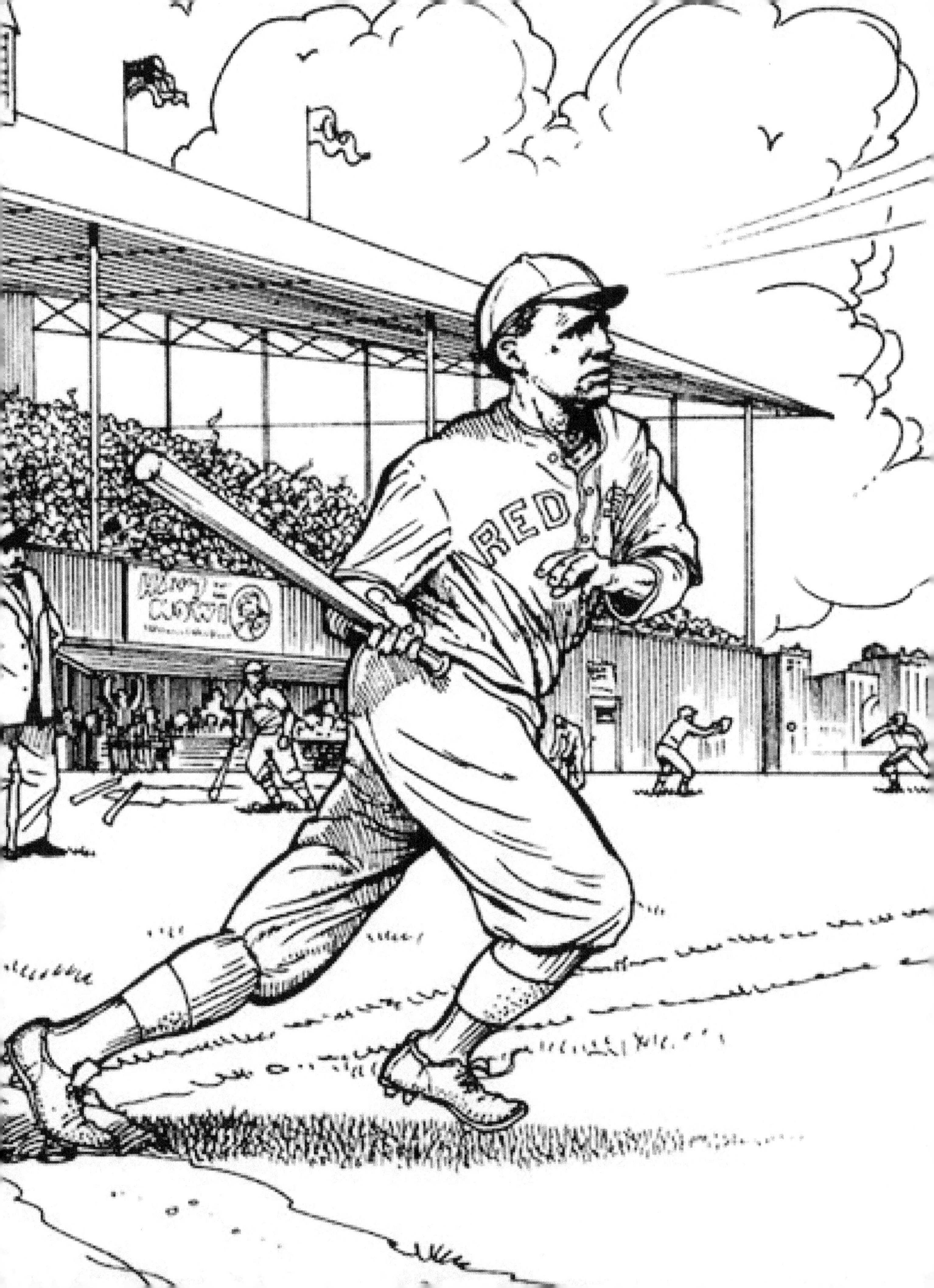
RED

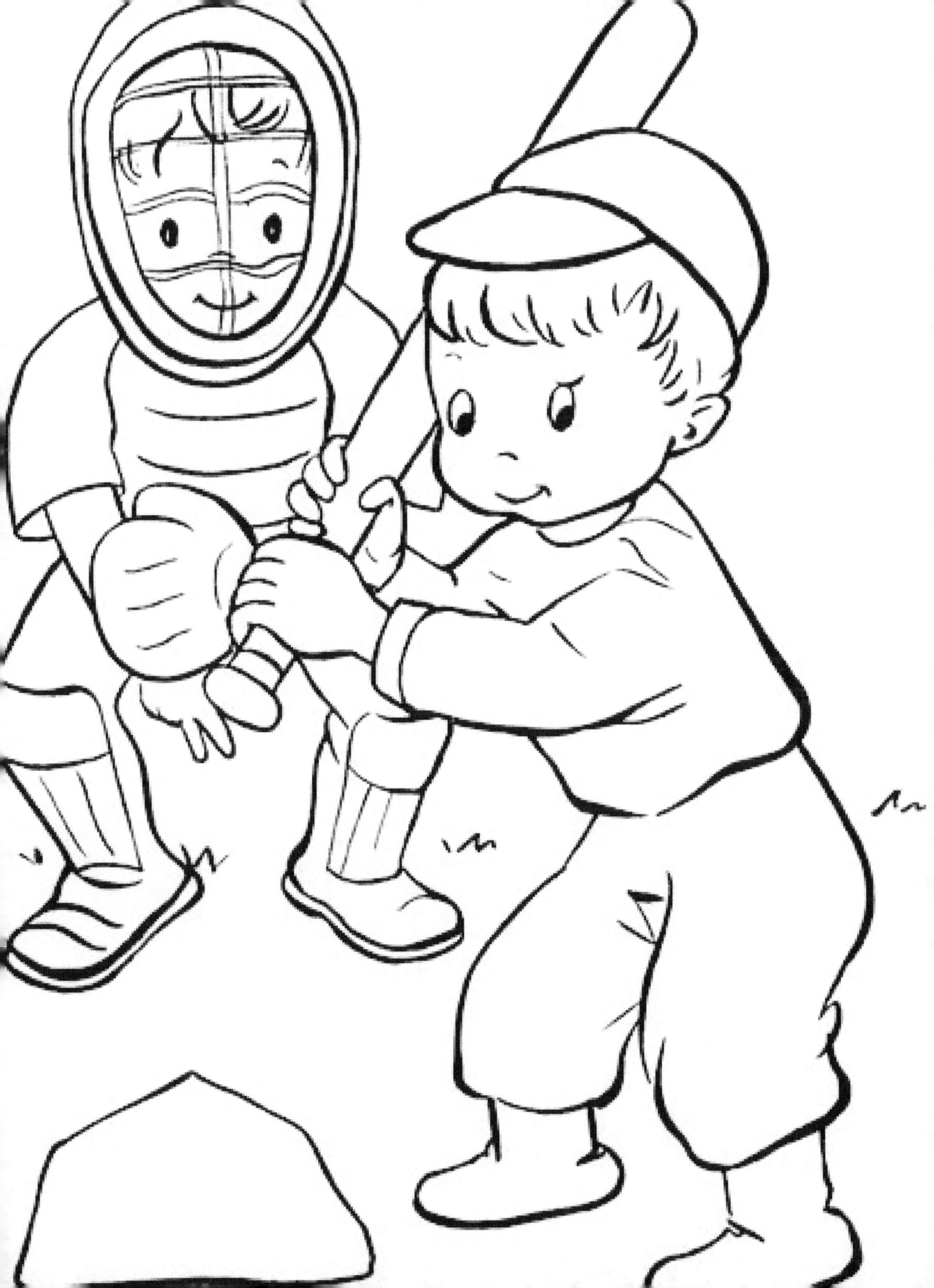

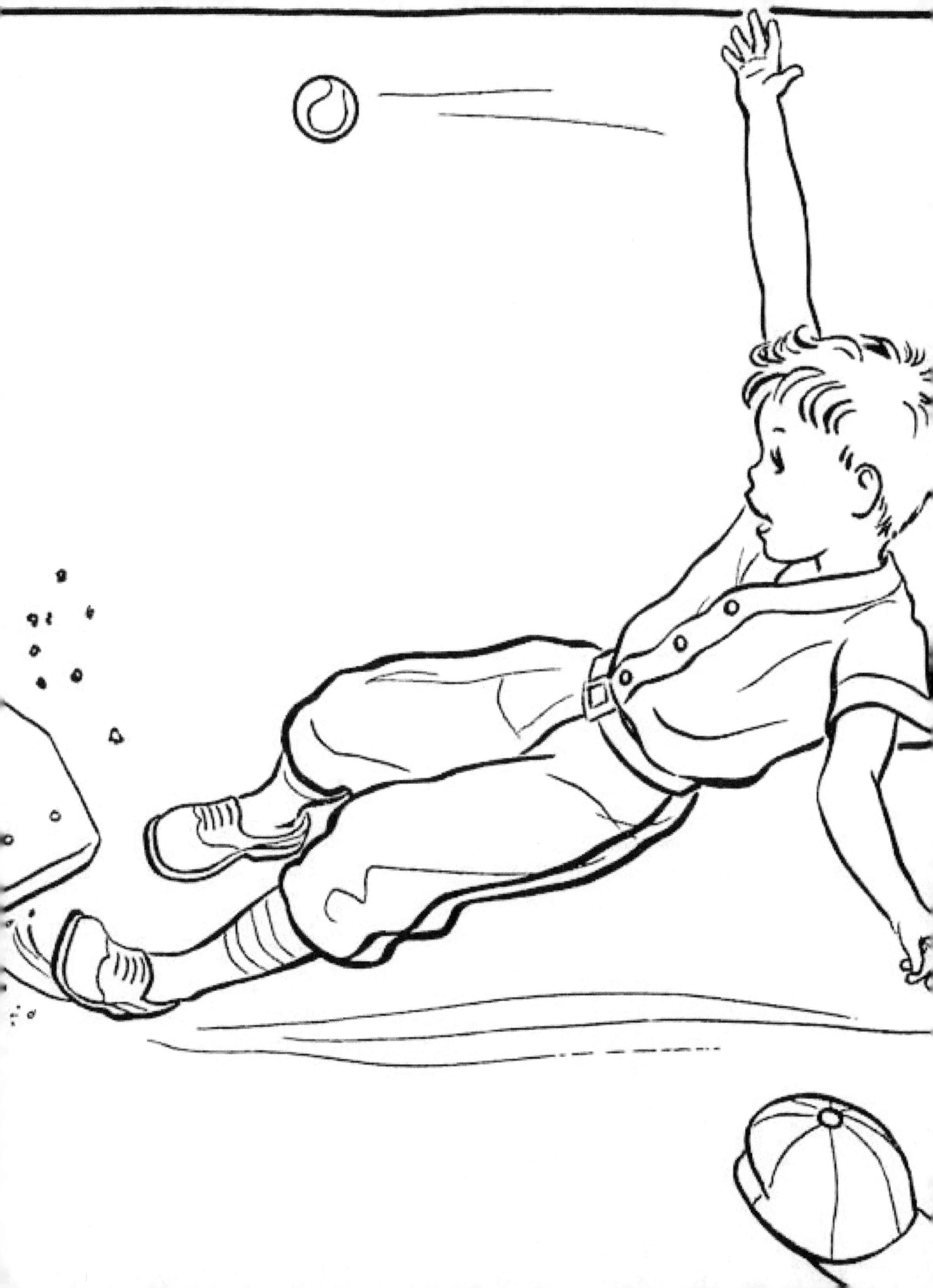

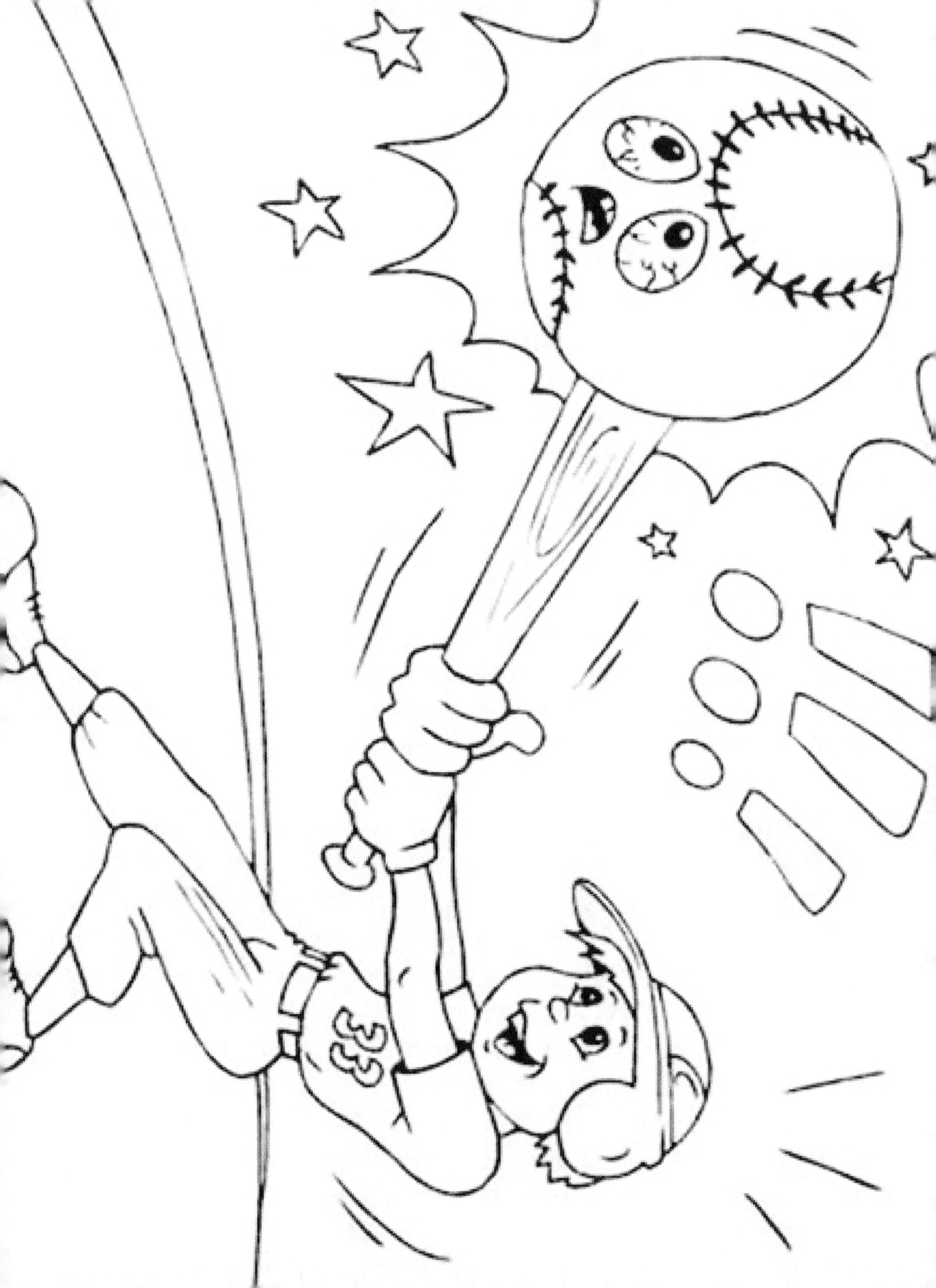
33

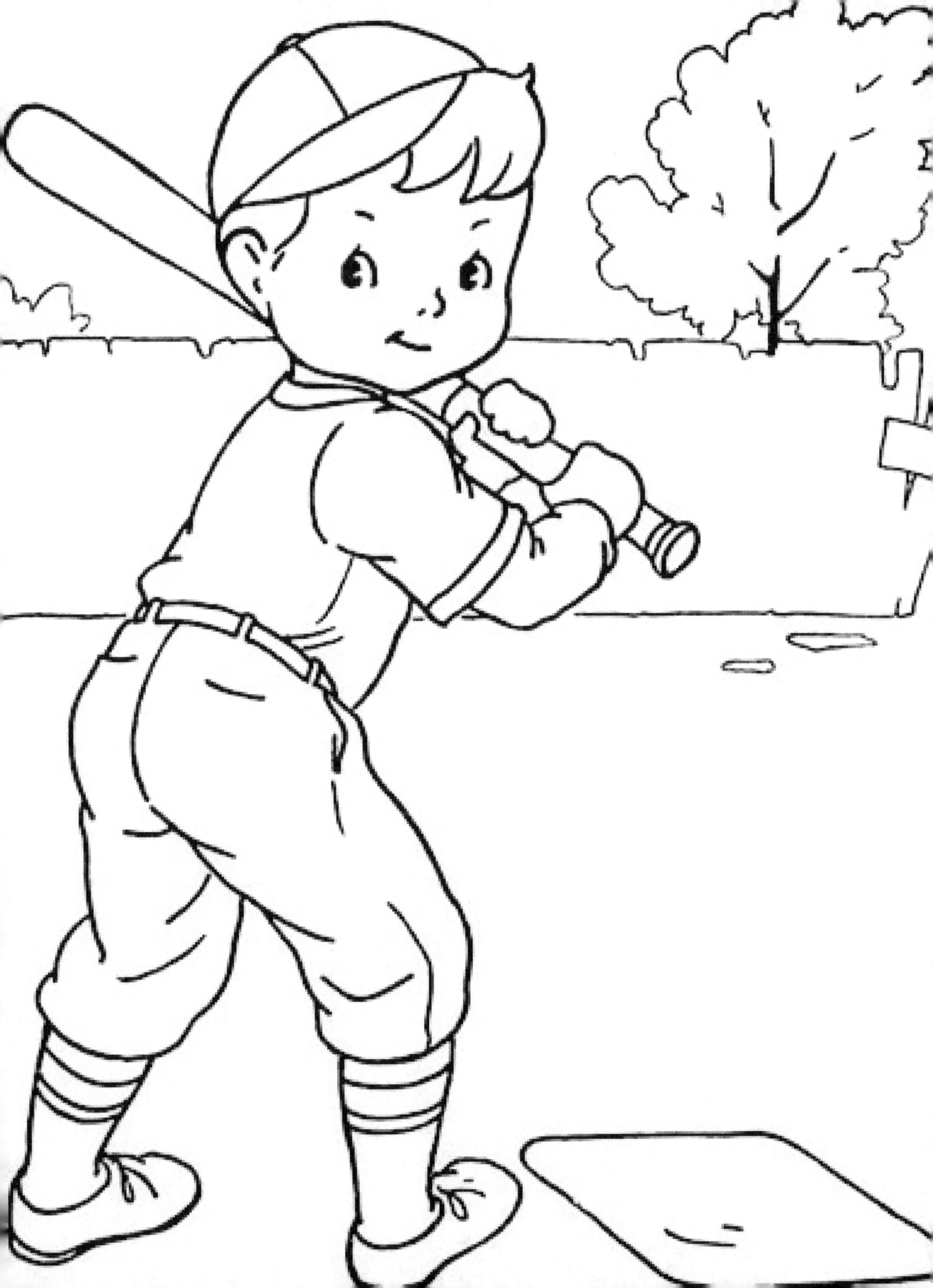

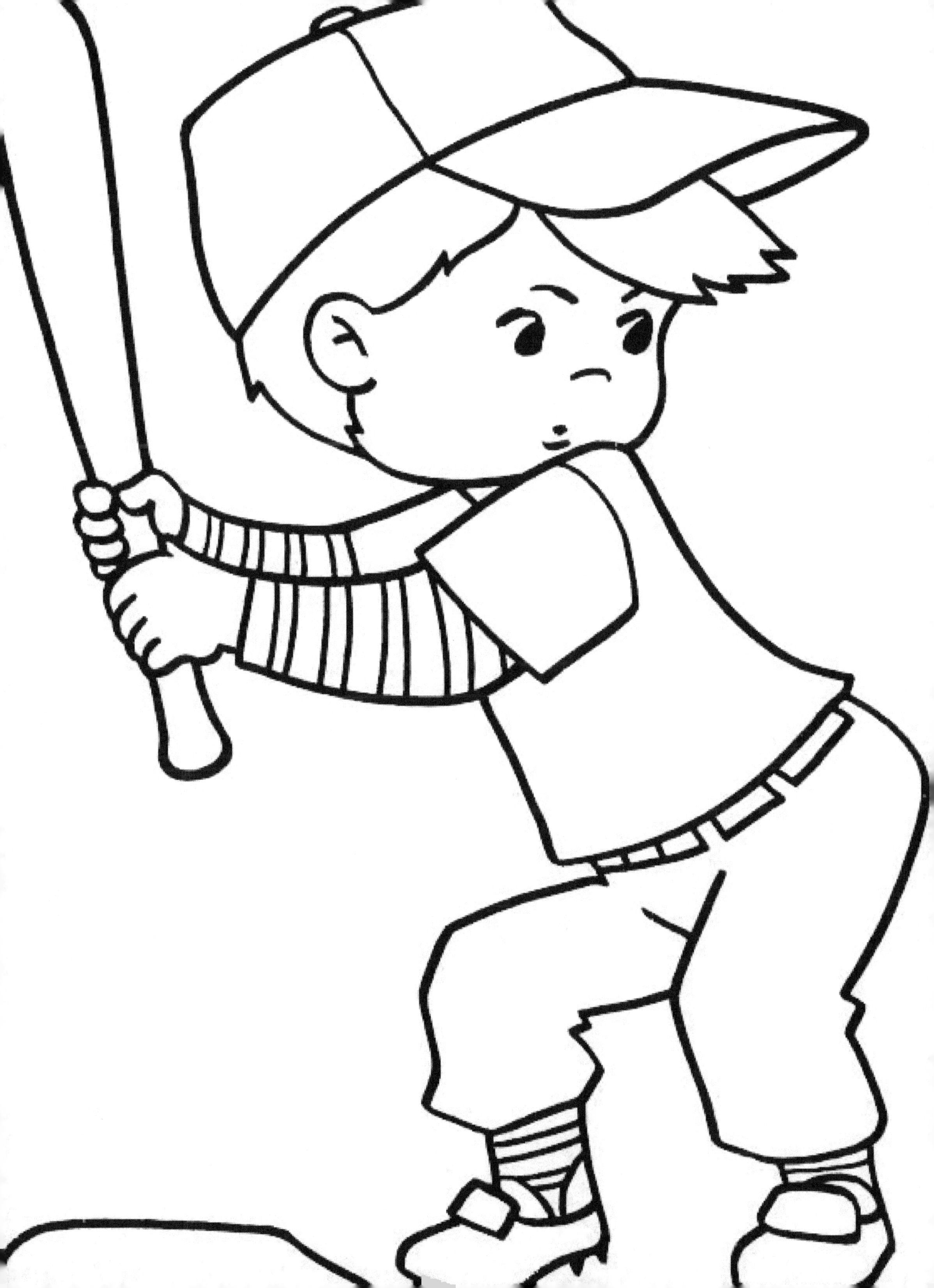

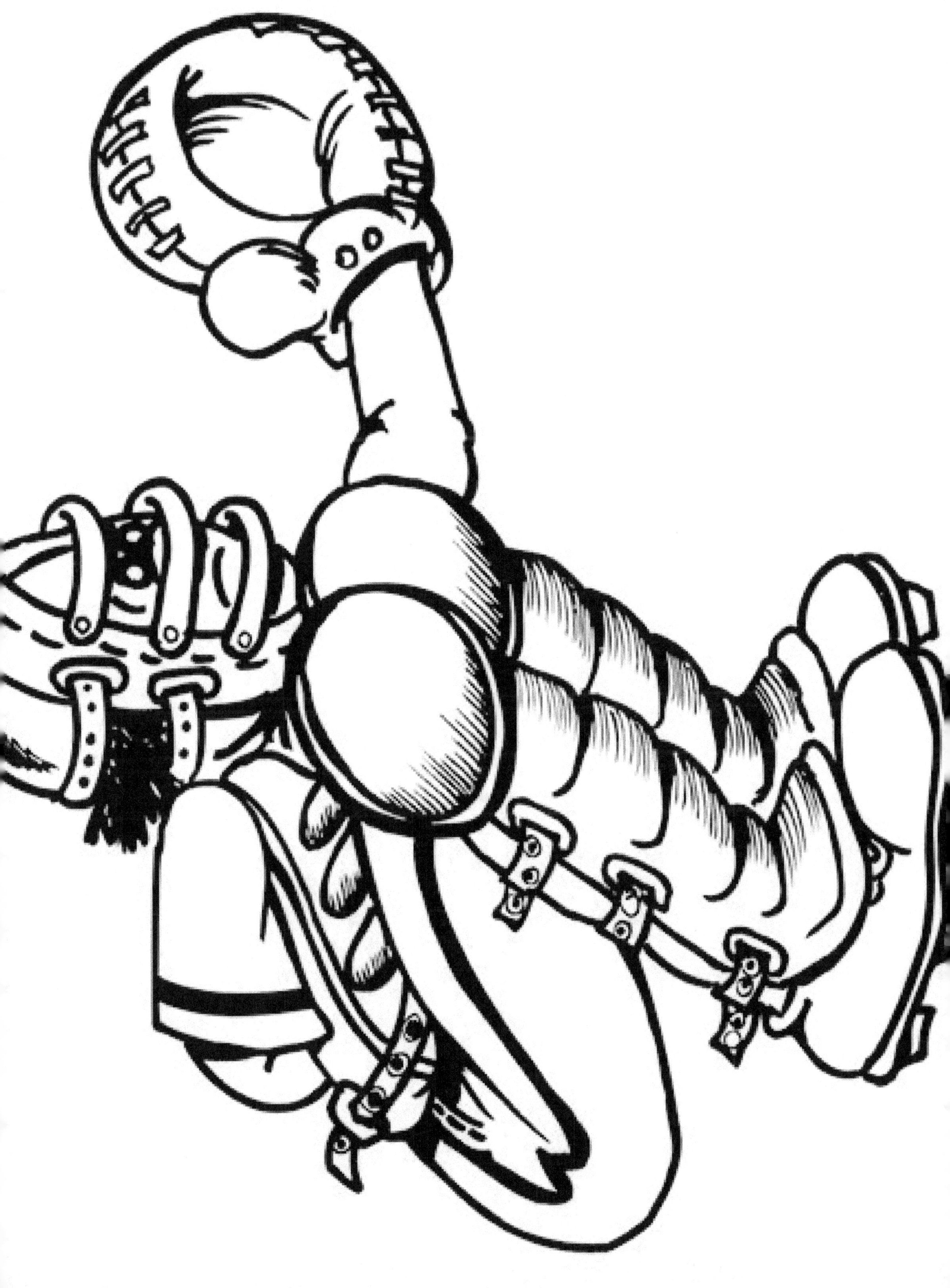

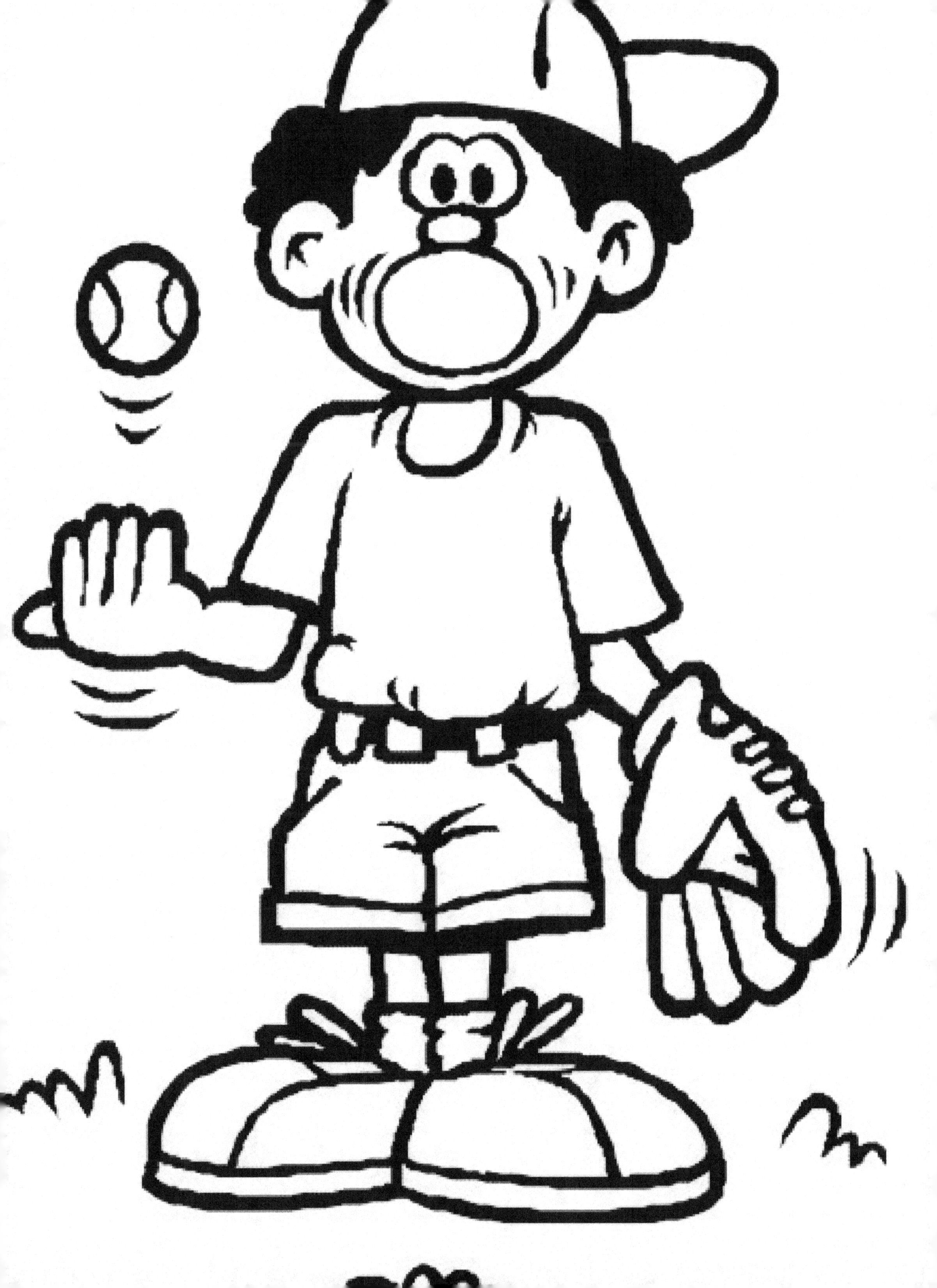

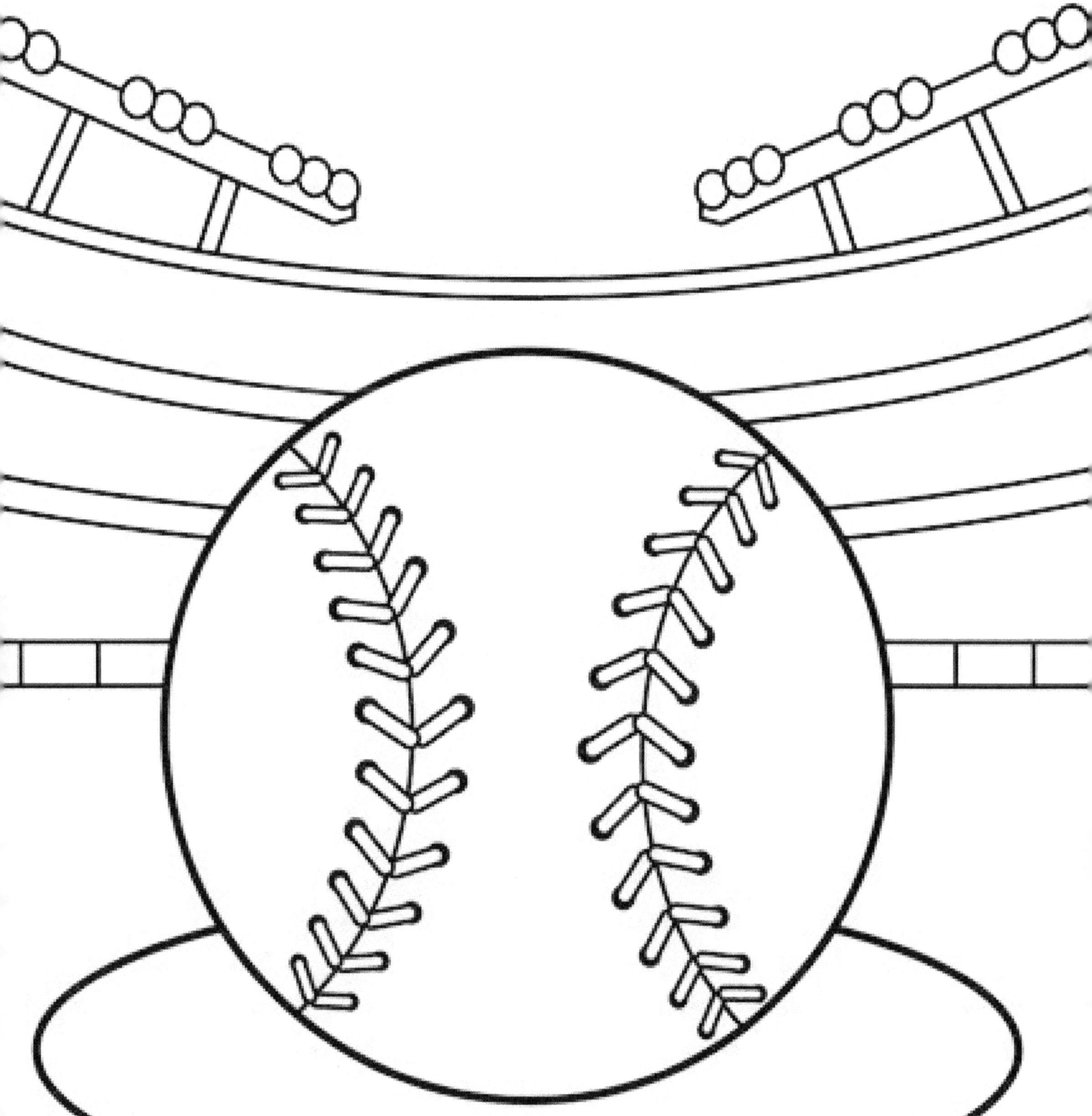

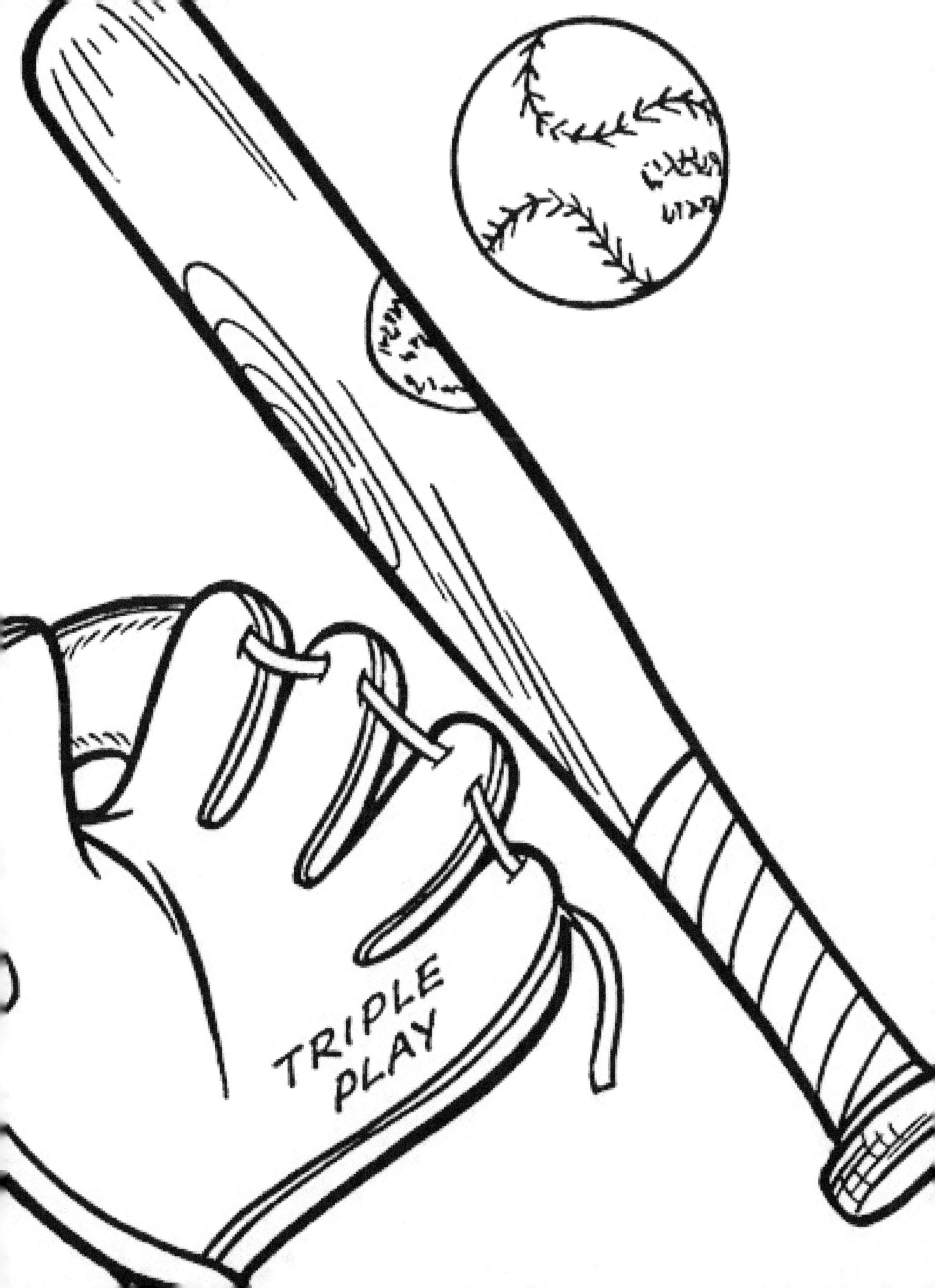
TRIPLE PLAY

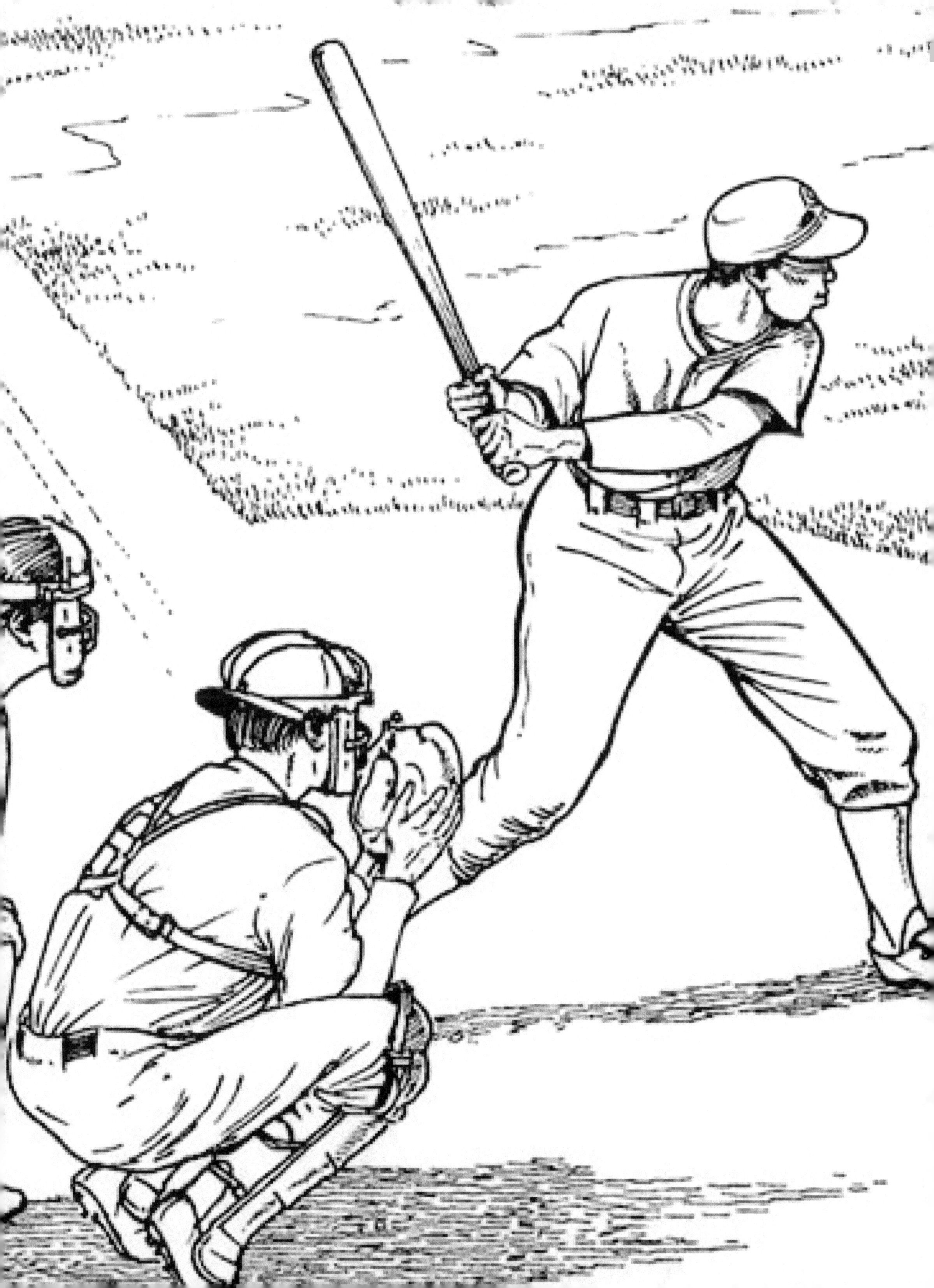

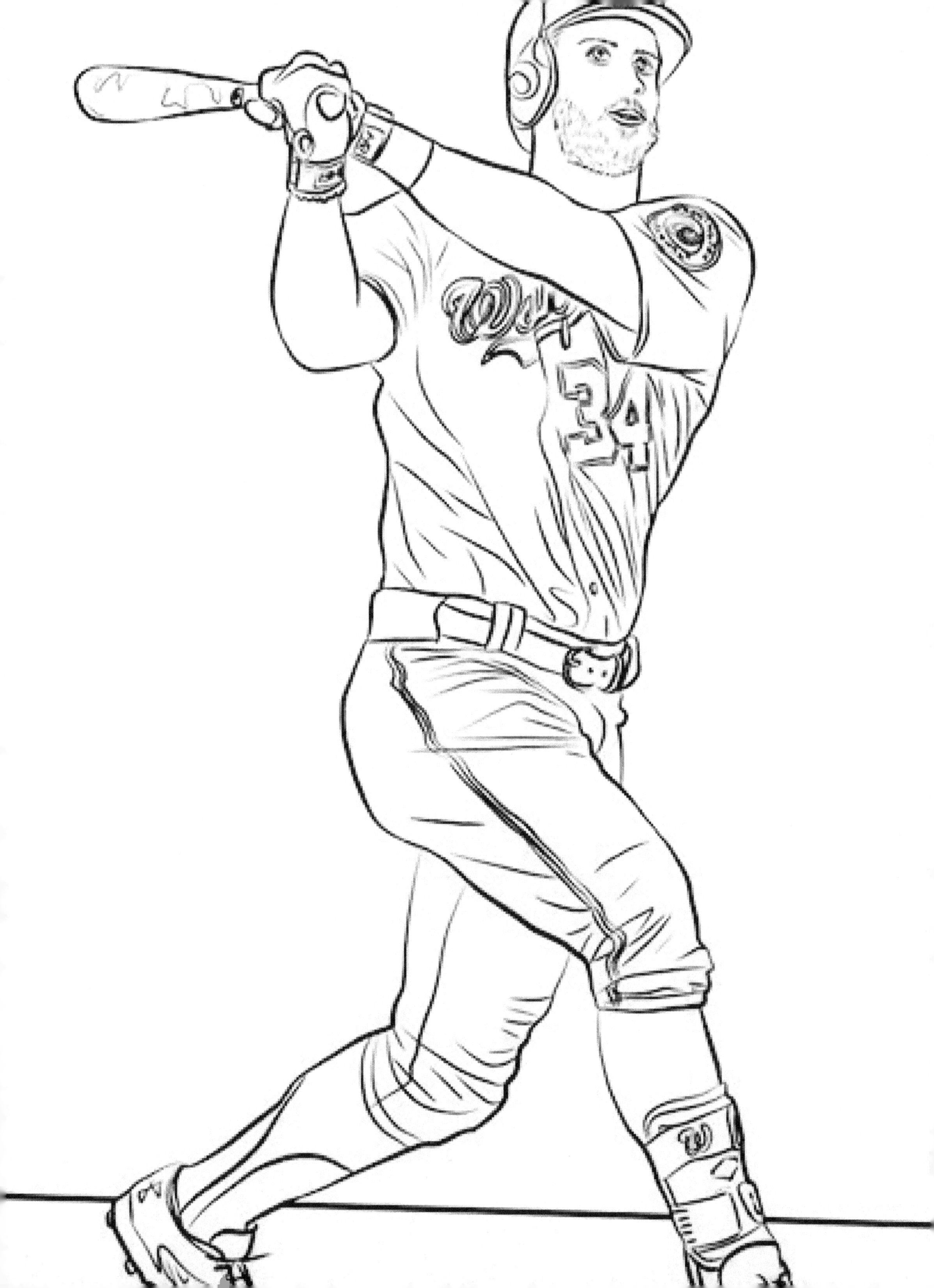
34

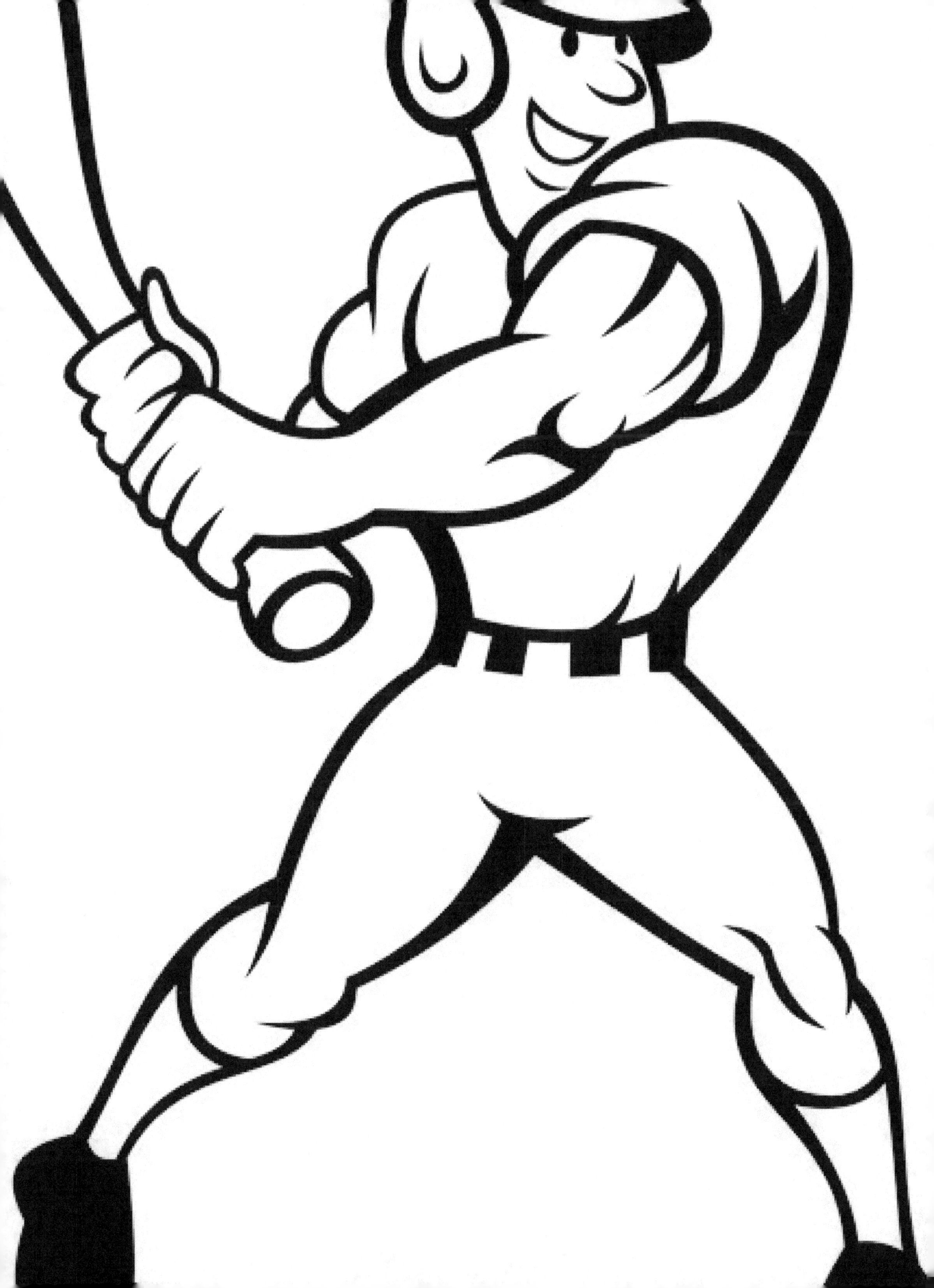

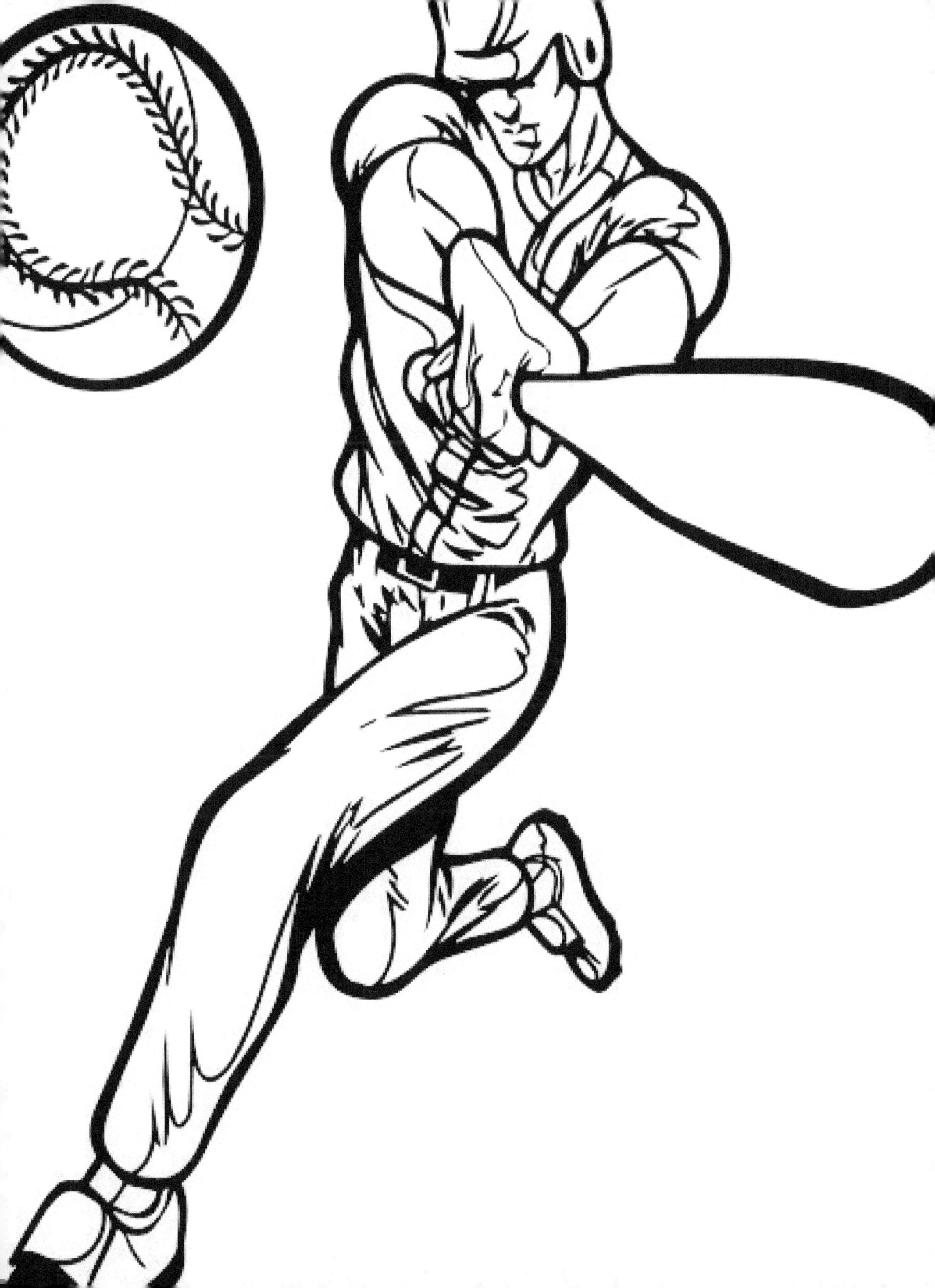

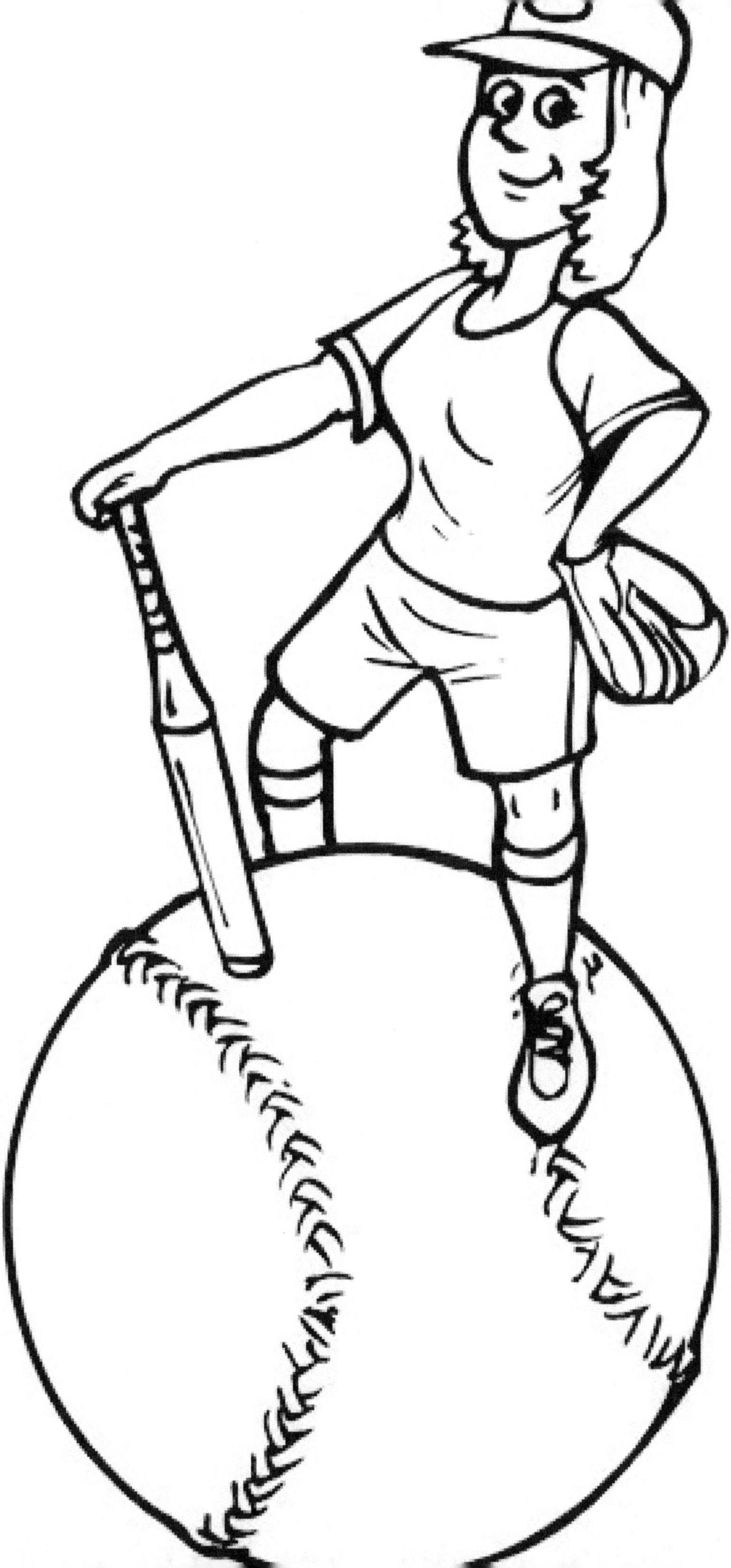

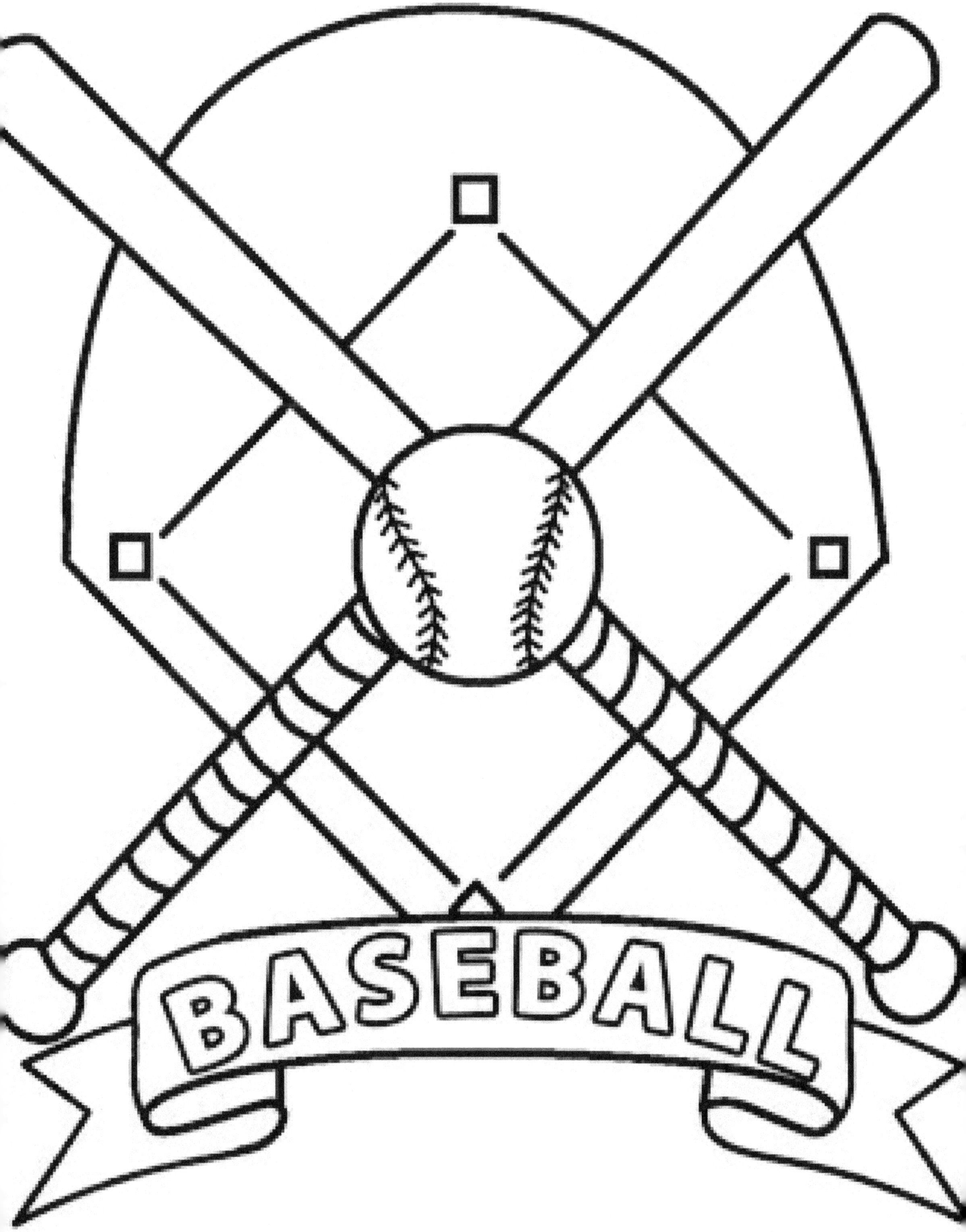
BASEBALL

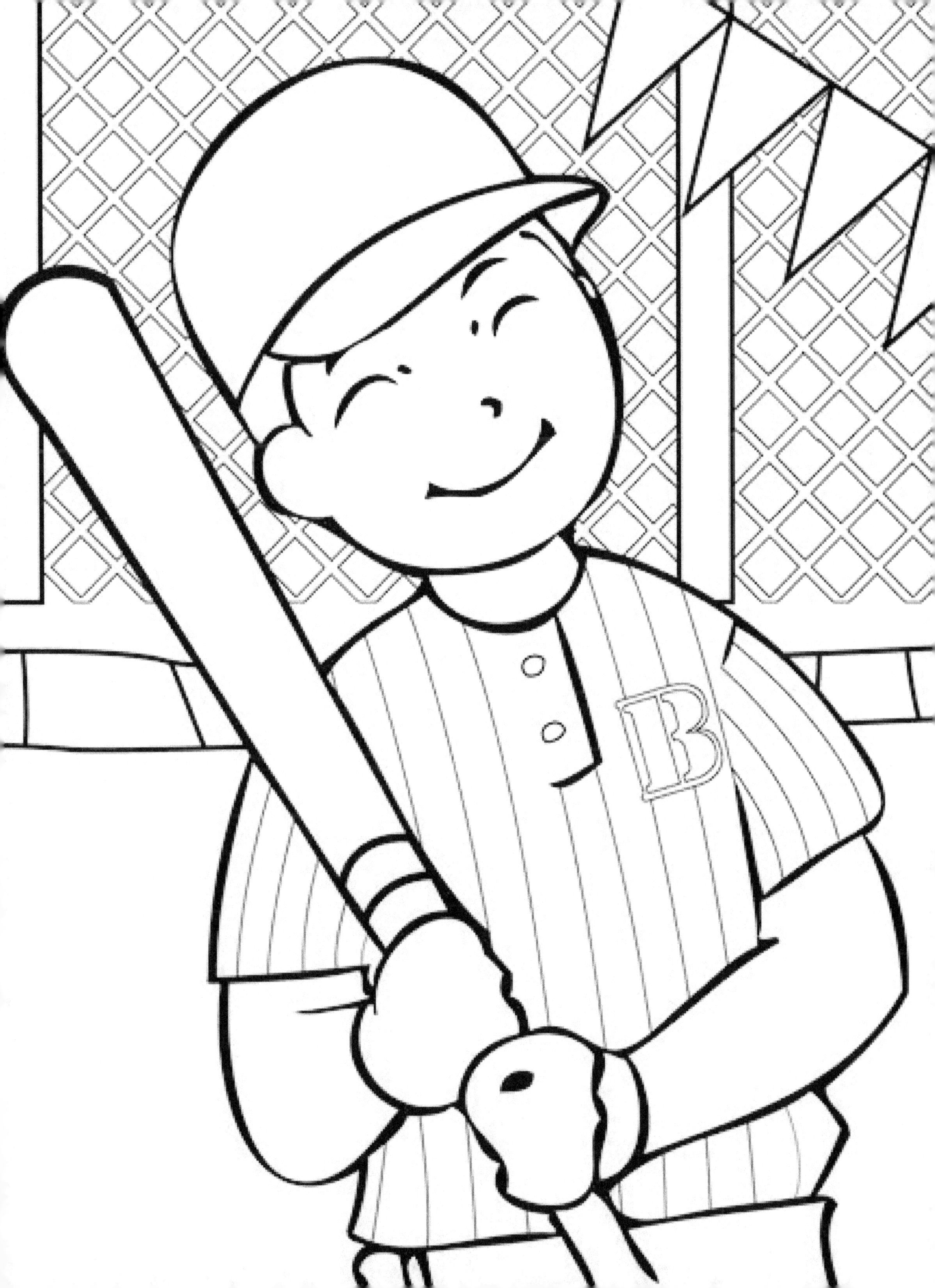
B

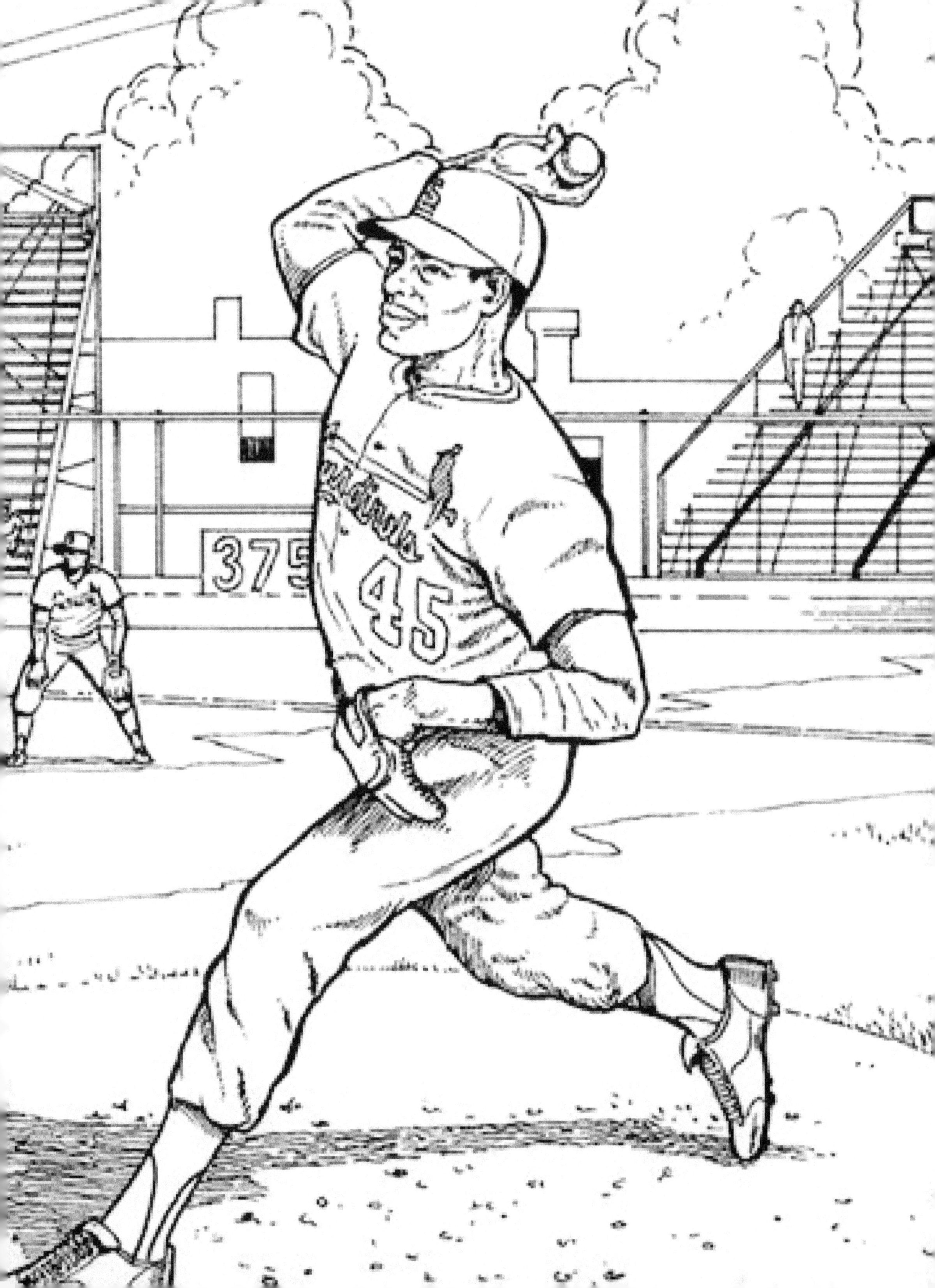
375
45

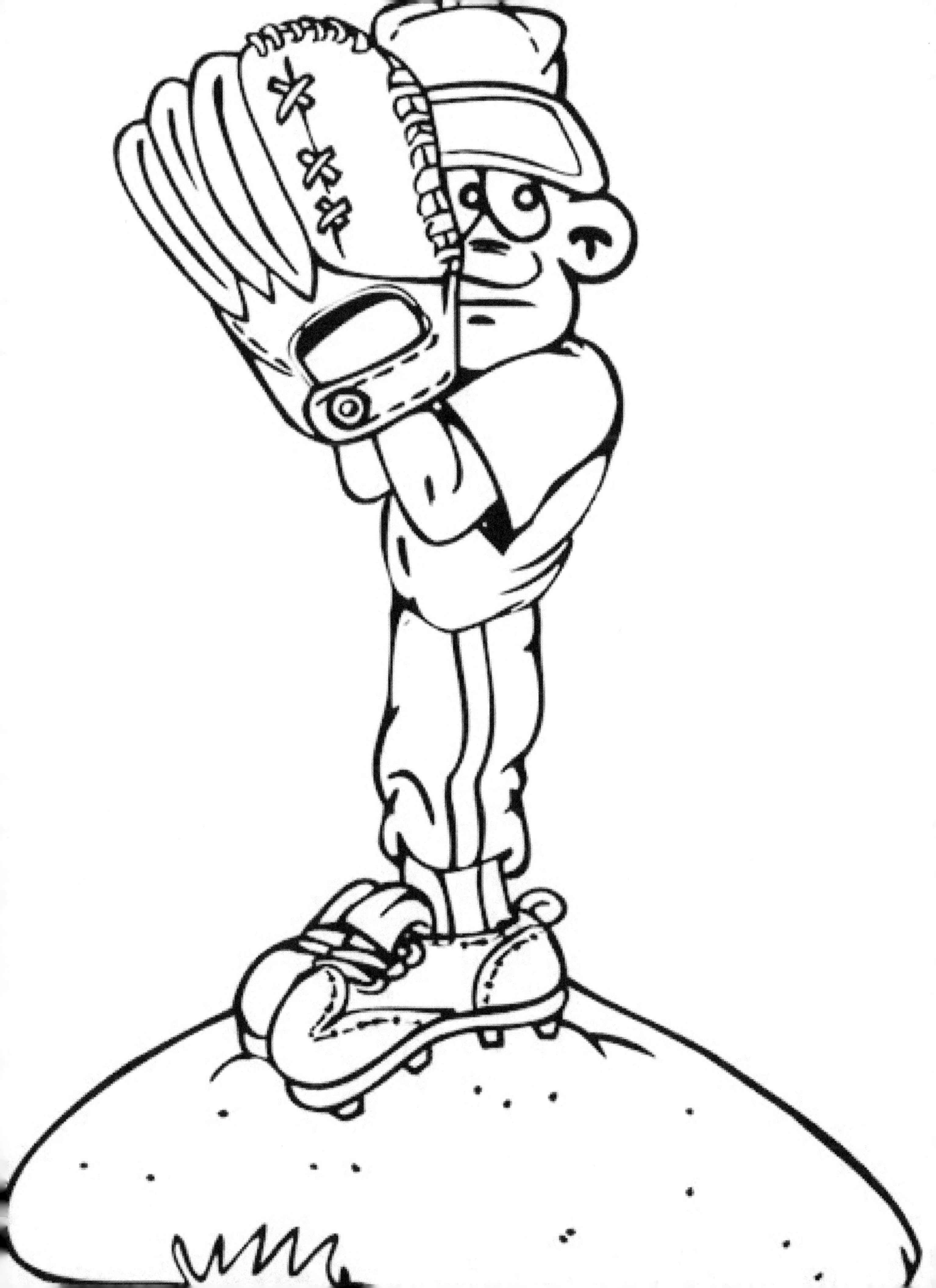

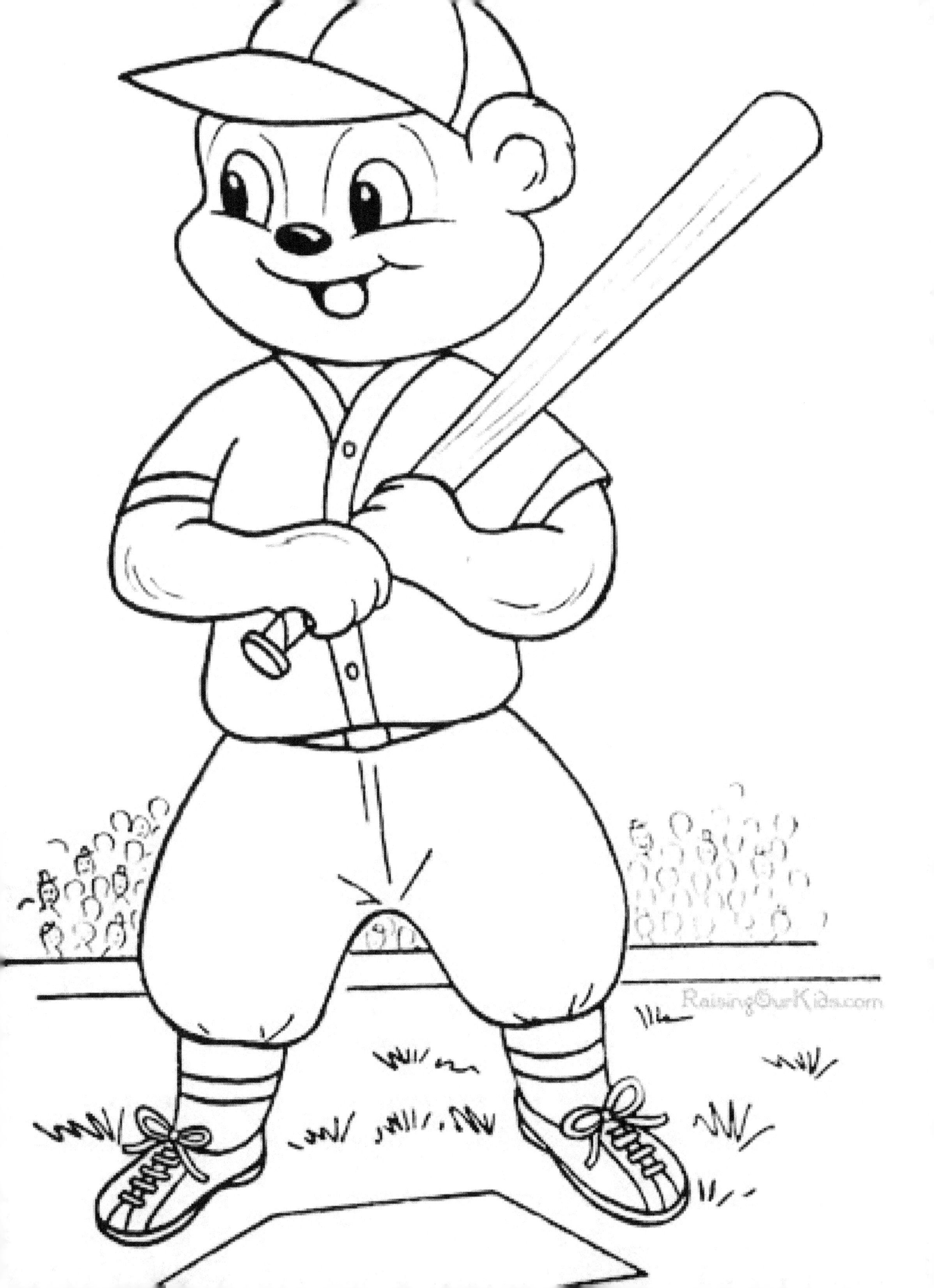
RaisingOurKids.com

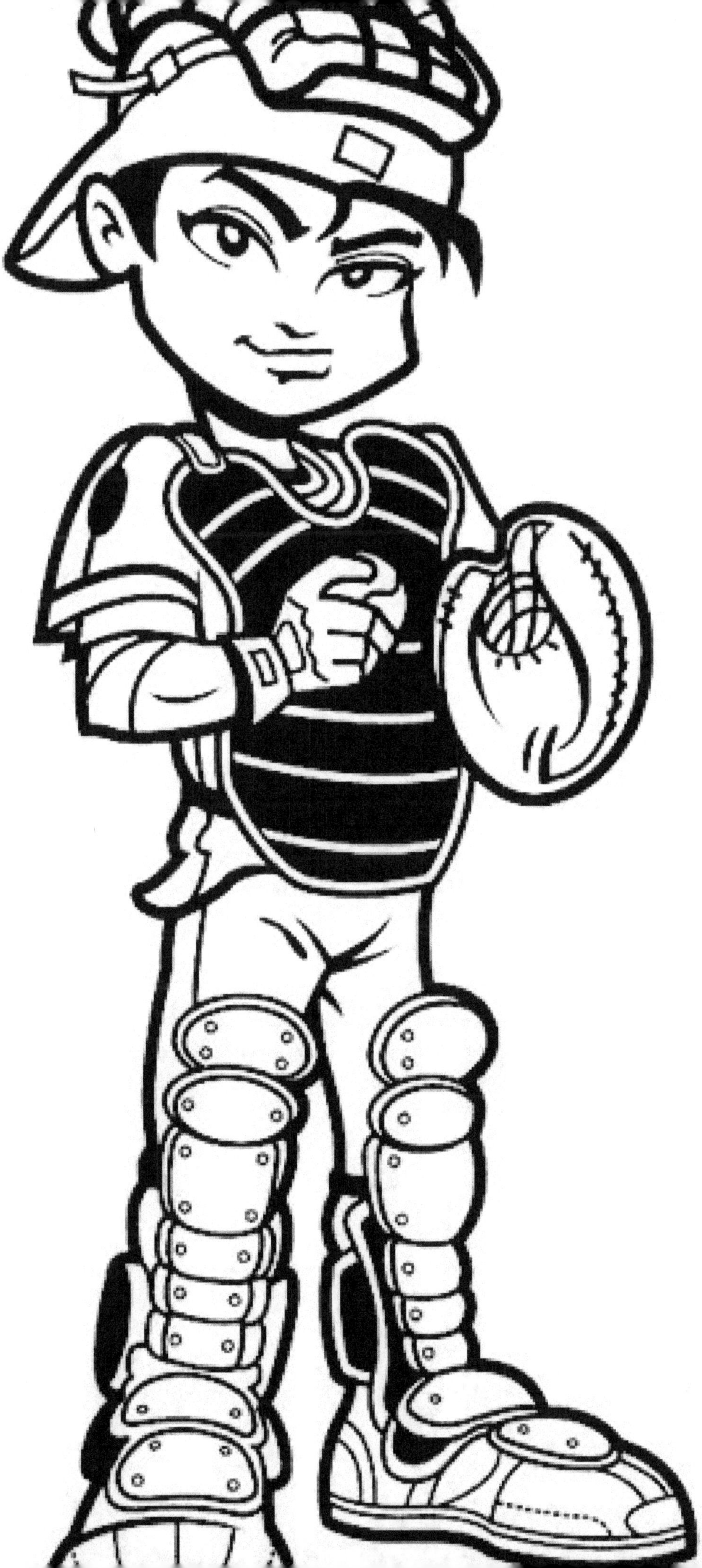

ORBIT

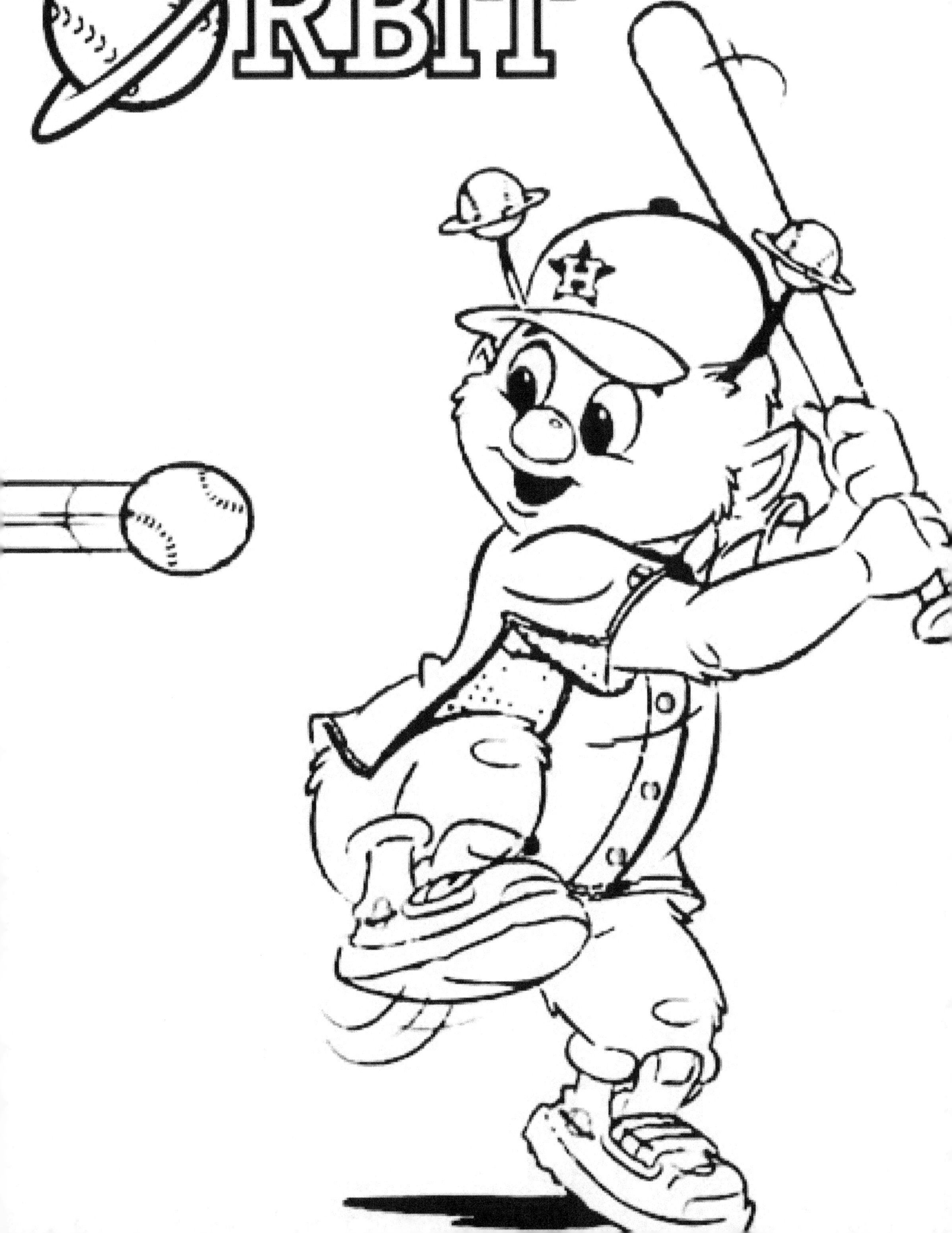

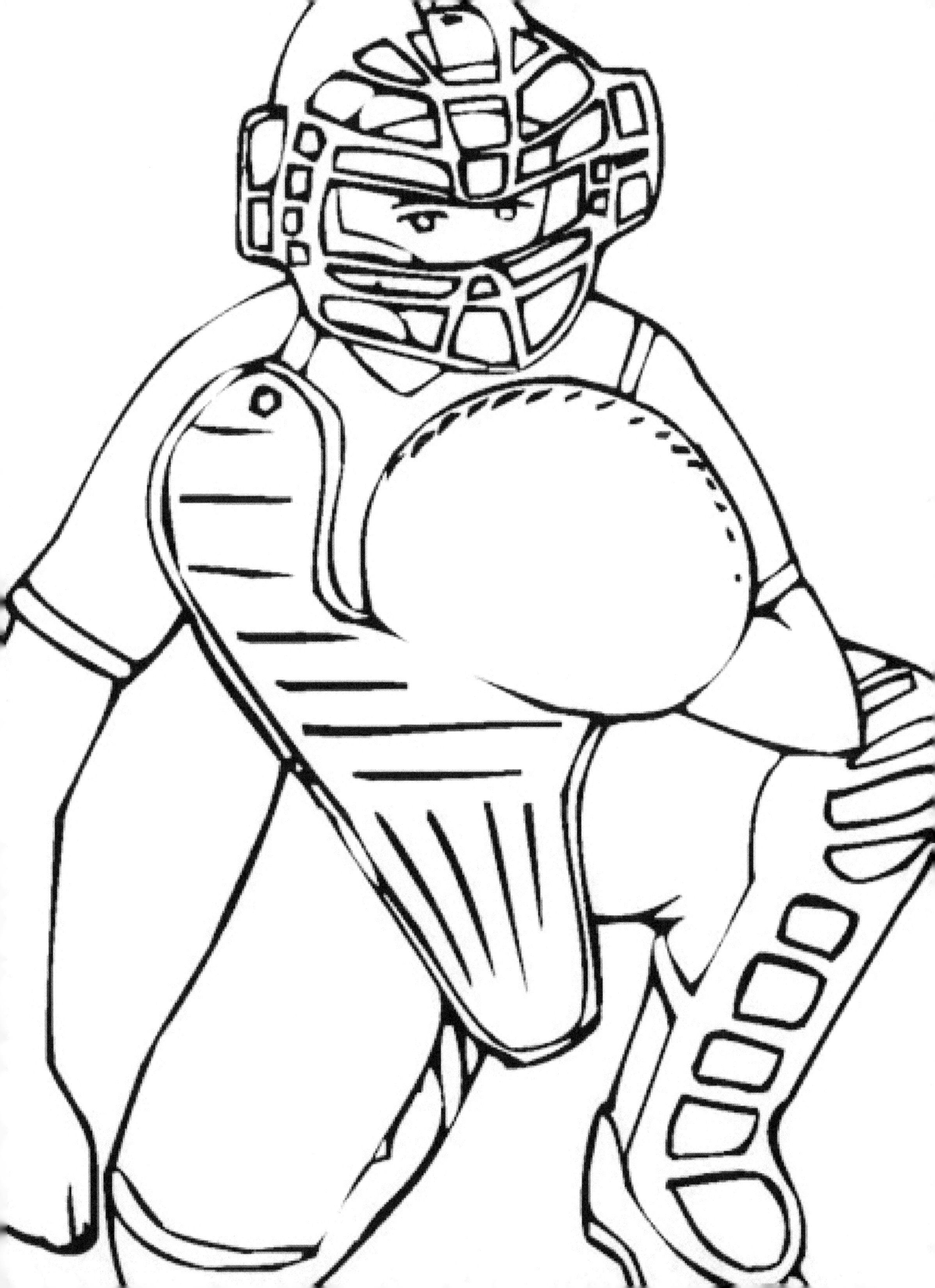

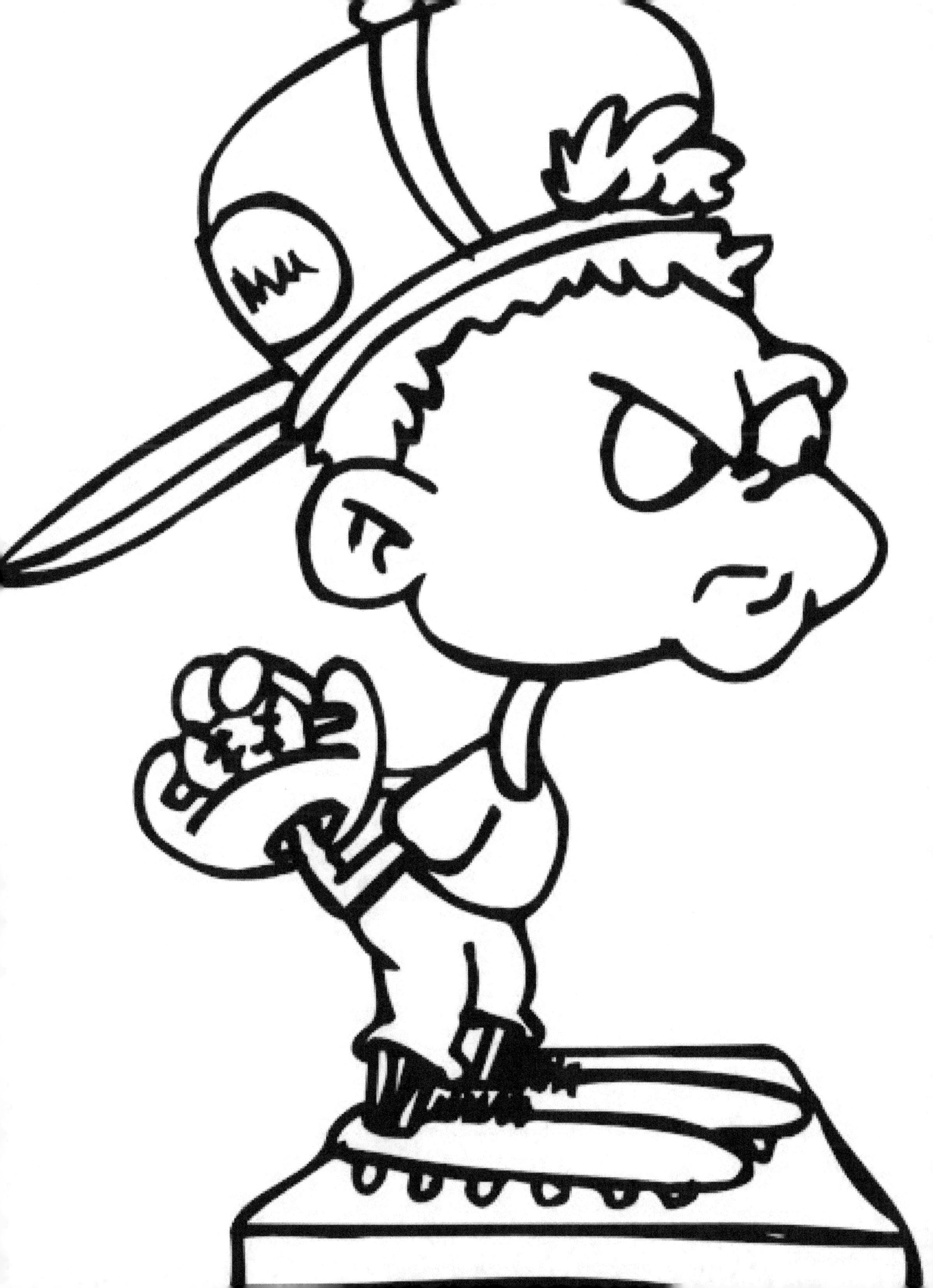

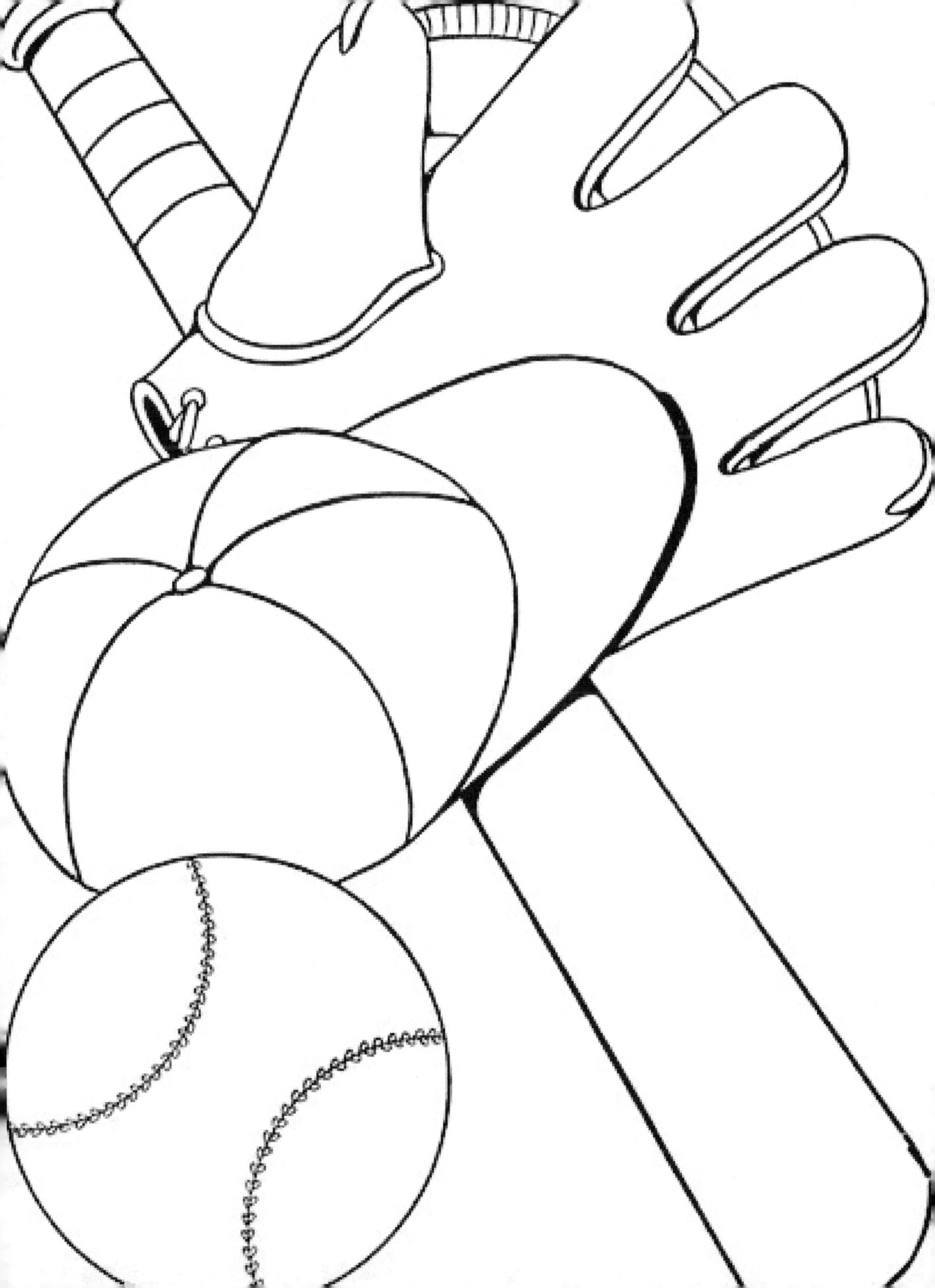

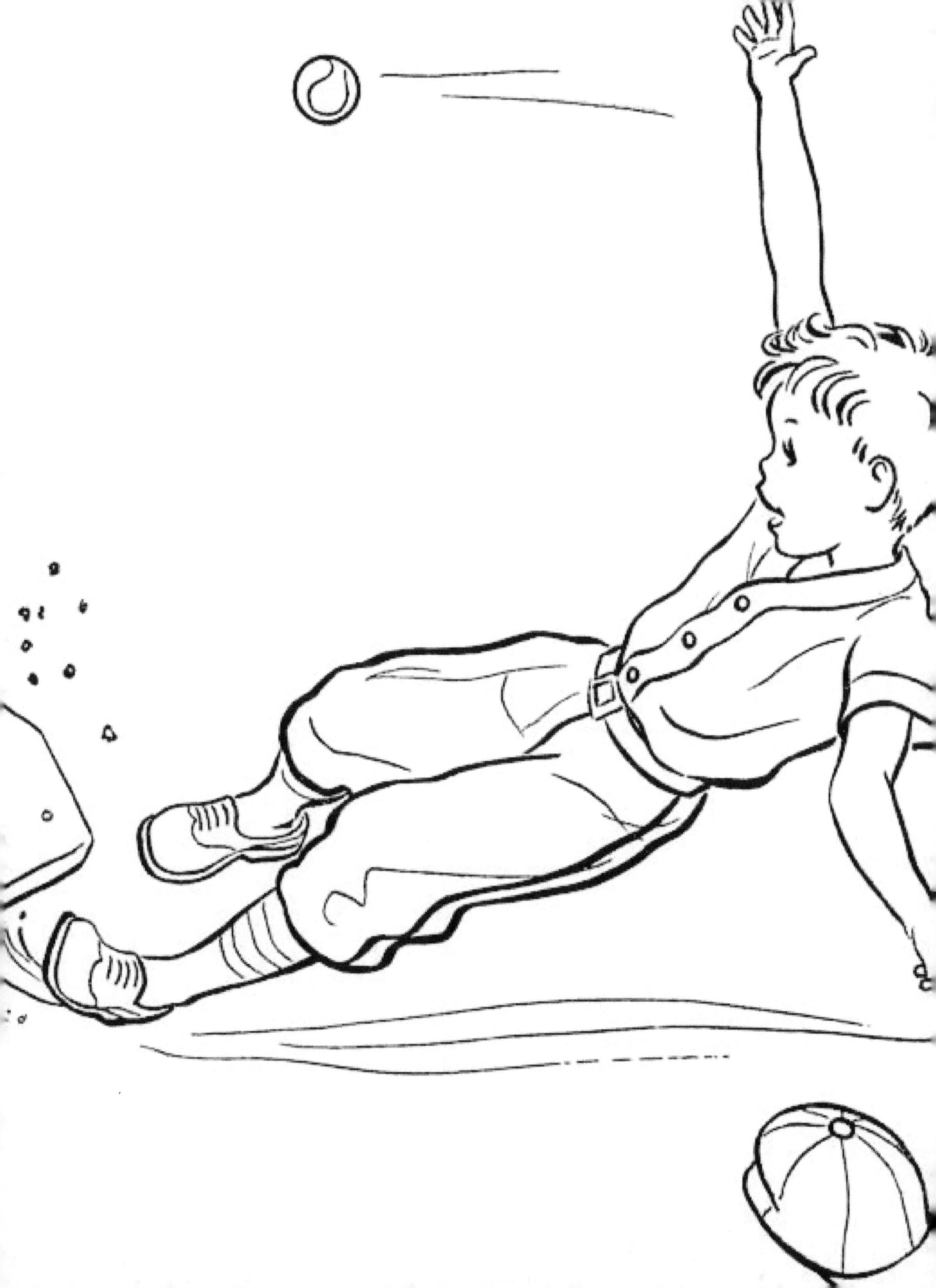

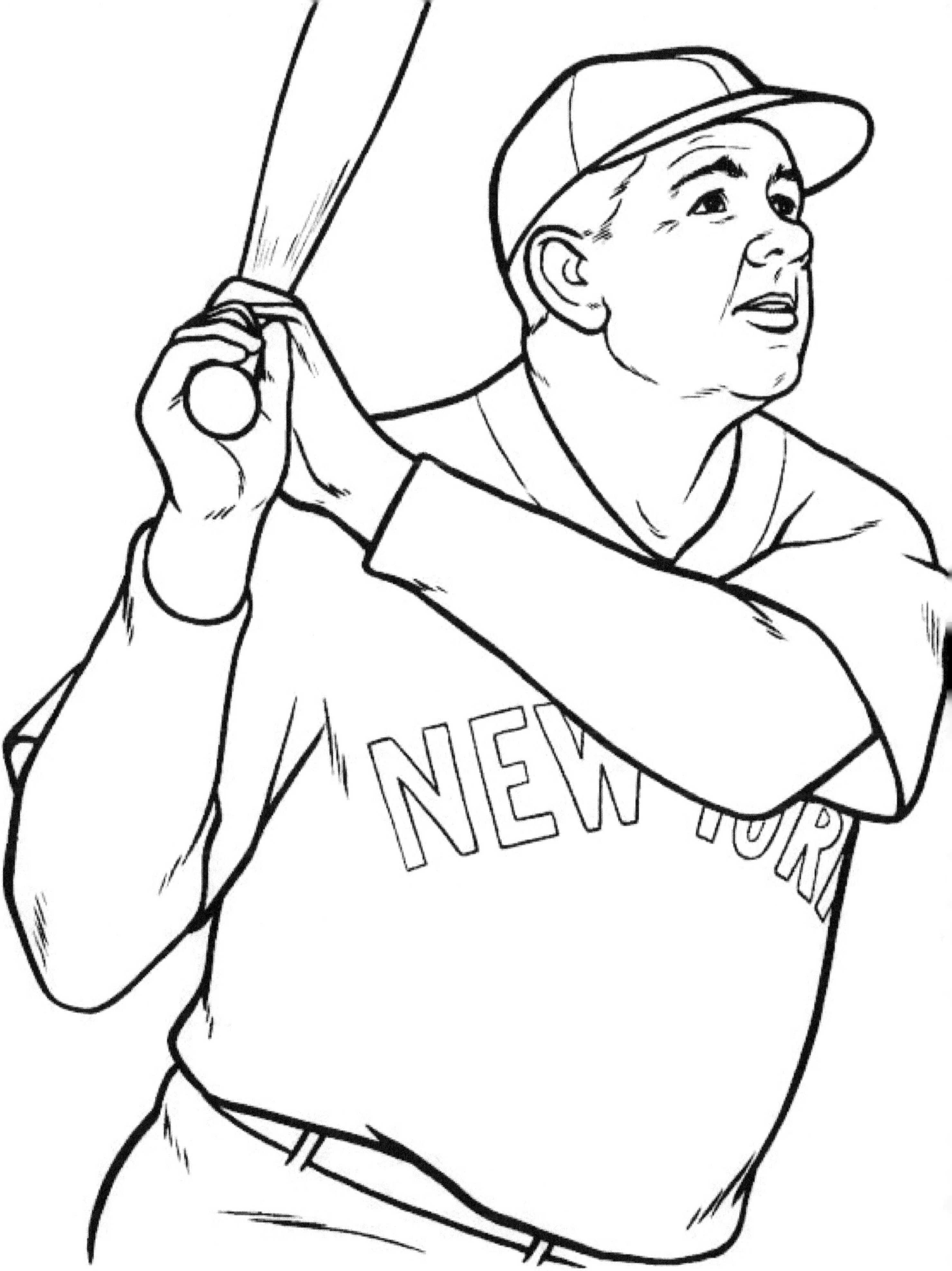
NEW

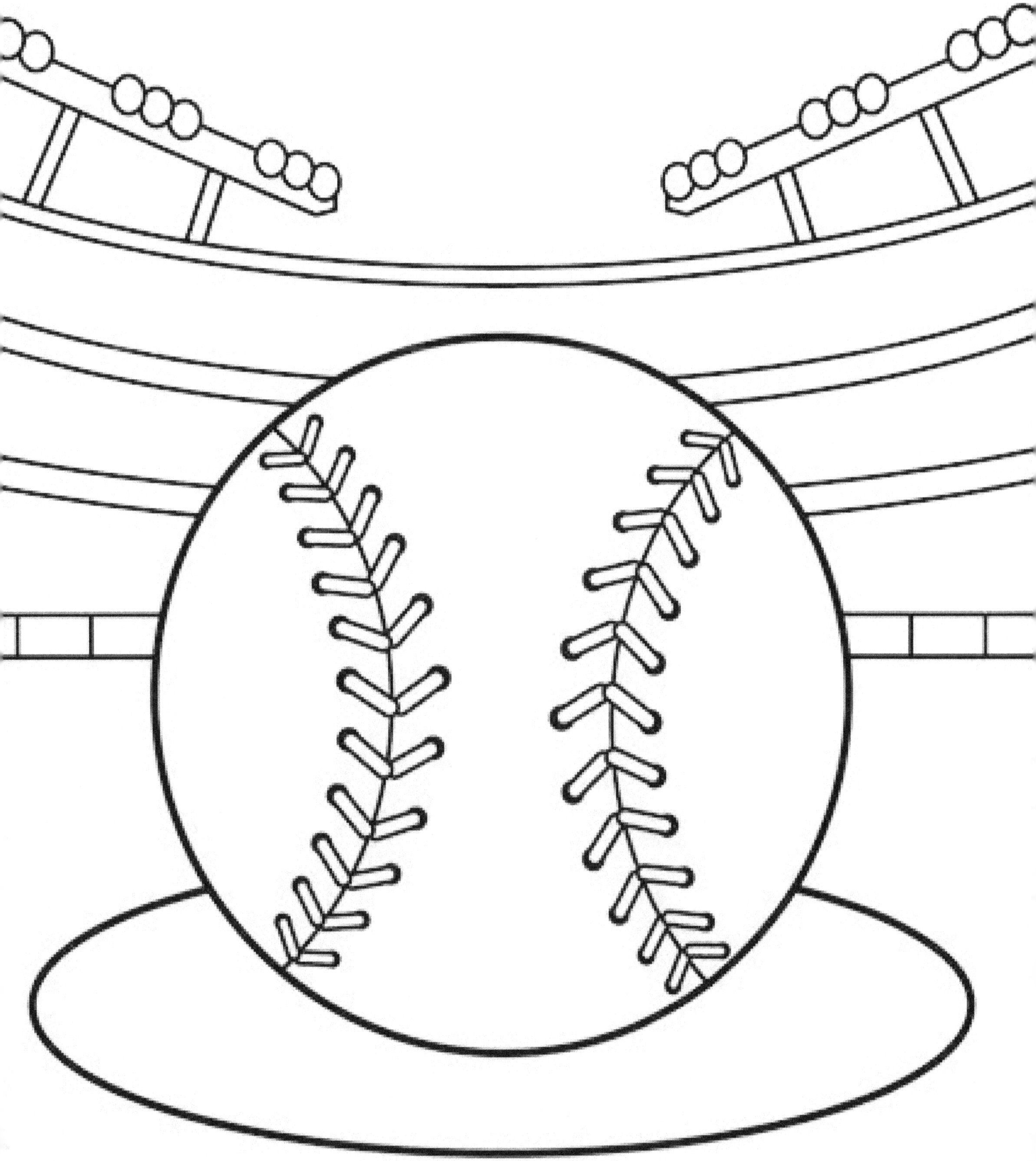

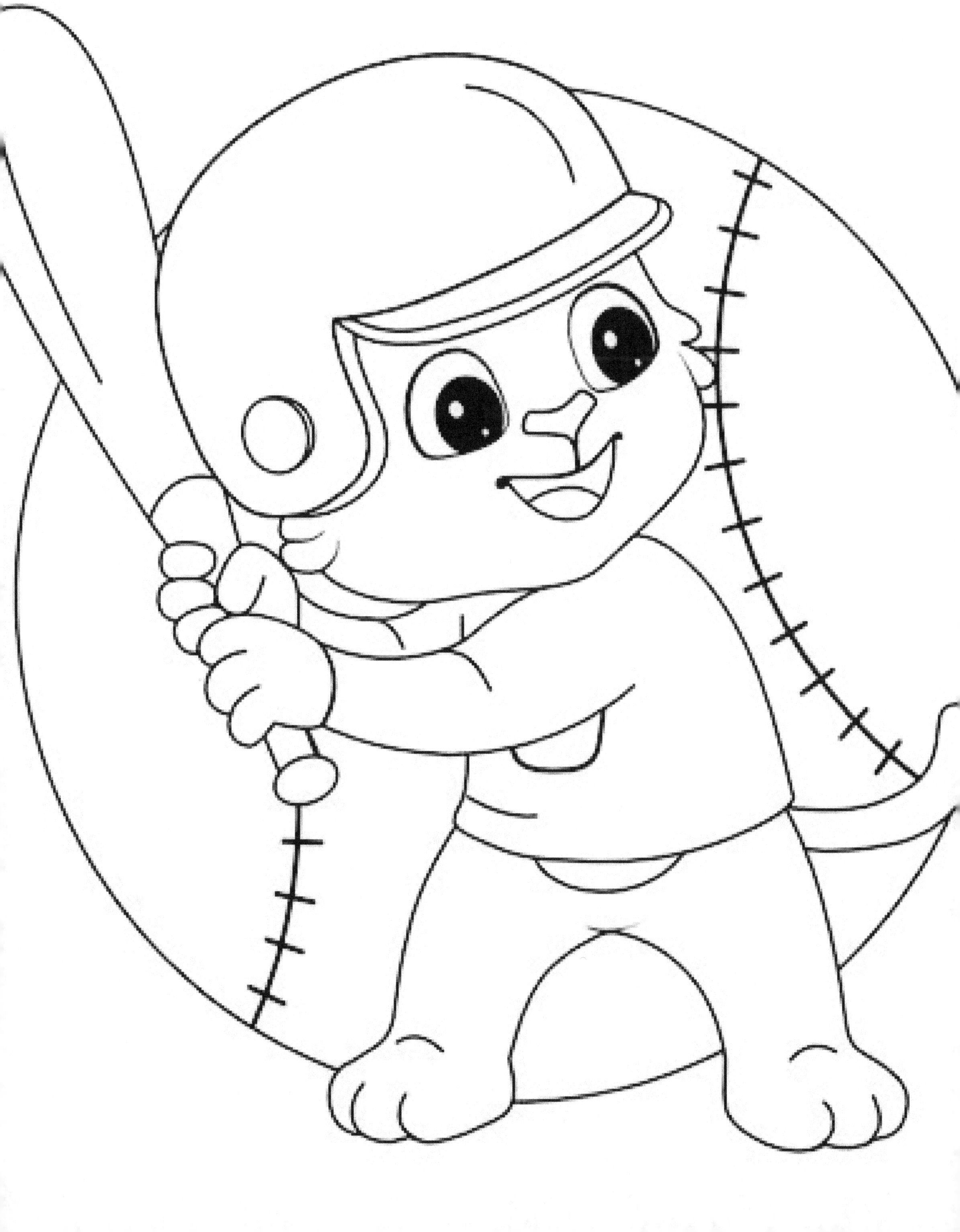

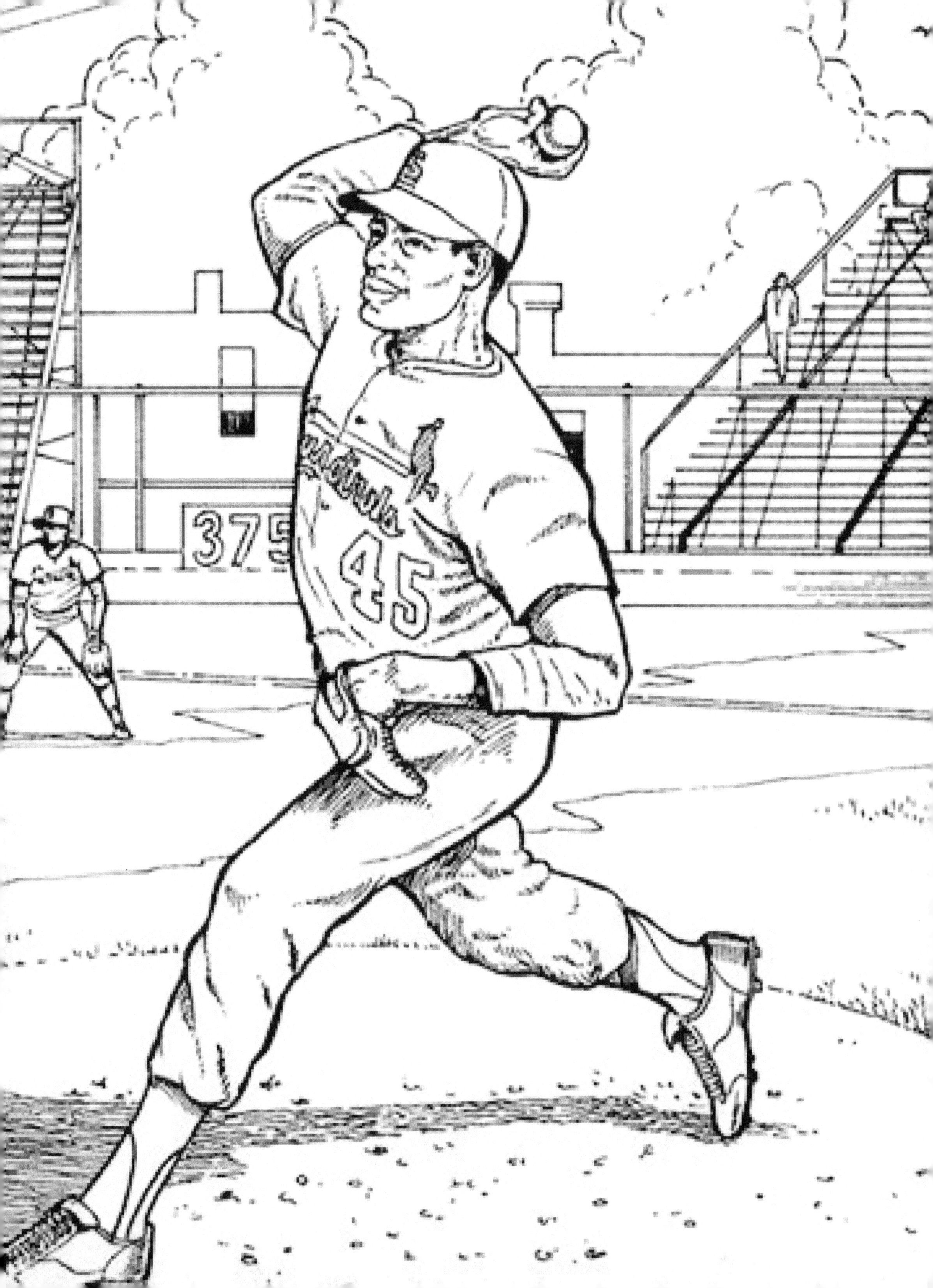
375
45

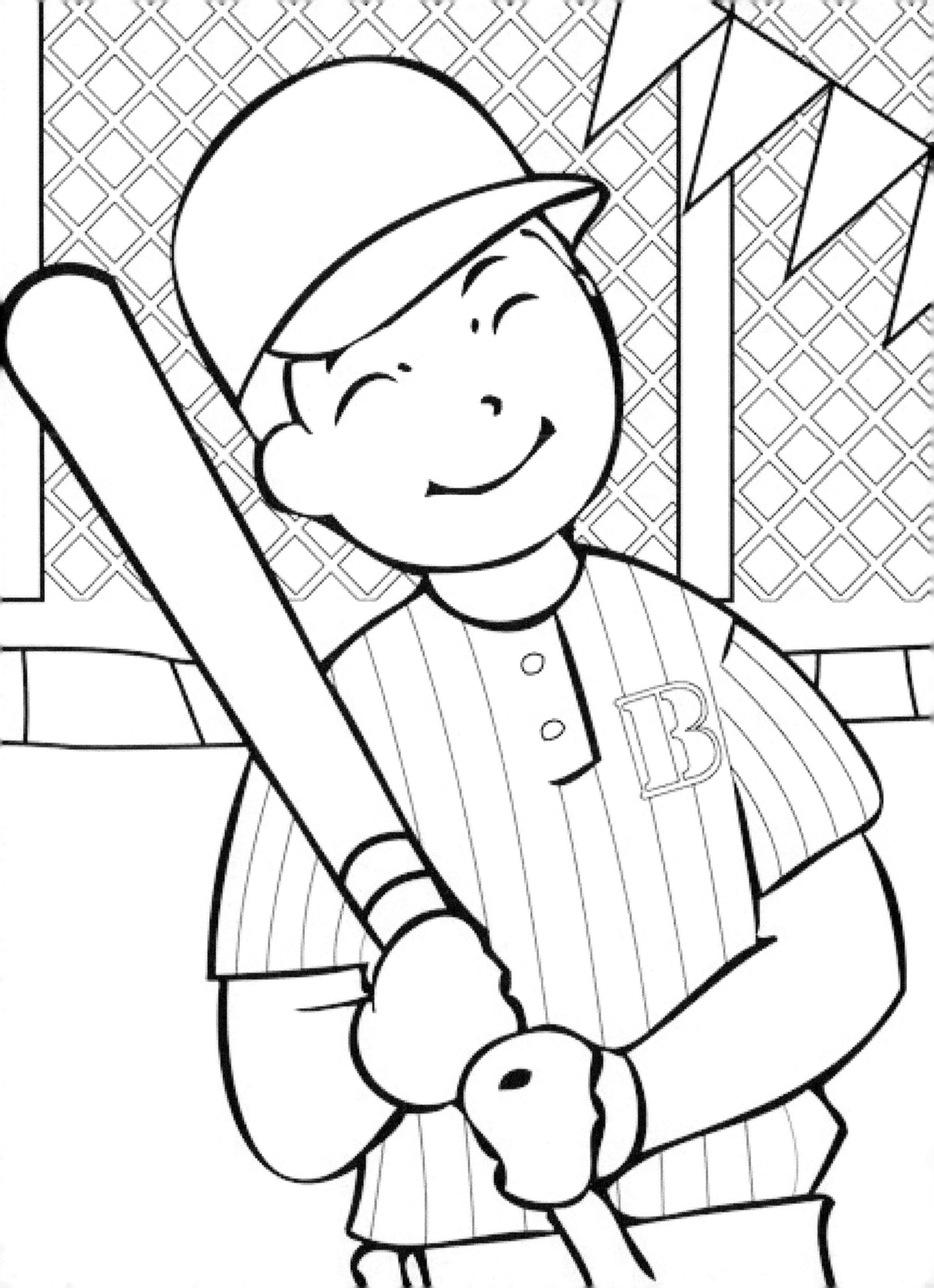
B

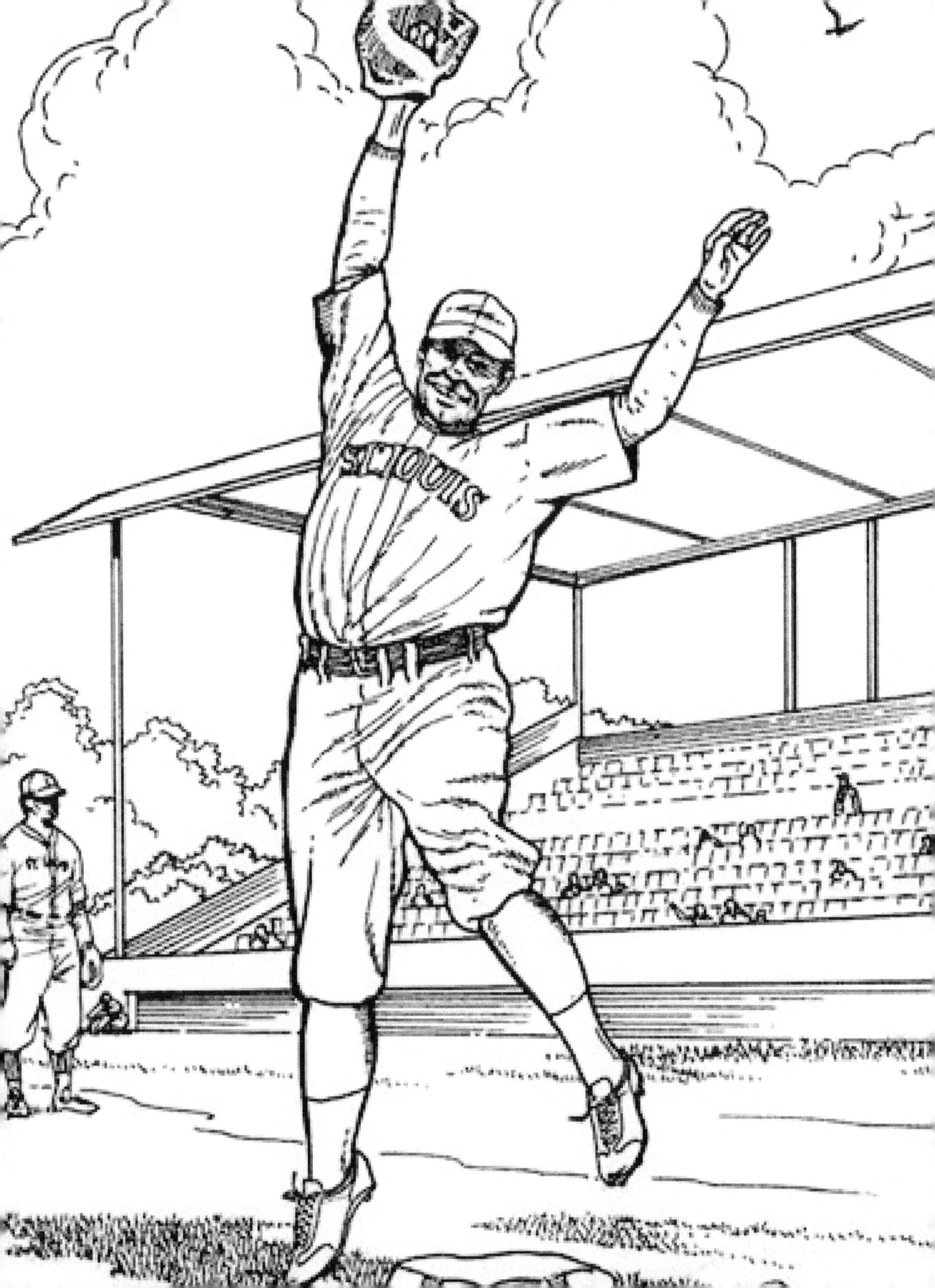
ST. LOUIS

www.ingramcontent.com/pod-product-compliance
Lightning Source LLC
Chambersburg PA
CBHW082224290526
45794CB00009B/3665
* 9 7 9 8 8 6 3 9 3 3 1 6 0 *